The Little Black Book of
Project
Management

The Little Black Book of Project Management

Michael C. Thomsett

amacom

American Management Association

Library of Congress Cataloging-in-Publication Data

Thomsett, Michael C.
    The little black book of project management / Michael C. Thomsett.
        p. cm.
    Includes index.
    ISBN 0-8144-7732-1
    1. Industrial project management.   I. Title.
HD69.P75T48   1990   90-55215
658.4'04—dc20   CIP

Printing number

10   9   8

Contents

The Little Black Book of Project Management

Introduction

Prediction is very difficult,
especially about the future.

—Neils Bohr

Imagine this situation: You've just been given the job of complet-
ing a very large project. Your sources are limited, your budget is
very small, and your deadline is very short. The precise goals of
the job have not been defined as well as you'd like, and you
don't know where to start.

This situation challenges your management skill on many
levels. You'll have to ask for a definition of just what you're
expected to achieve. Then you'll need to plan well enough so
that you will accomplish the desired result, by the deadline and
within budget. Rarely will you be given a well-defined, fully
budgeted project and asked merely to pilot your resources
through to the end result. More likely you will be given an
assignment that includes nothing beyond the demand for a
generalized end result. The rest is up to you.

This Little Black Book shows you how to take charge of a big project,
define it, and then break it down into smaller, more manageable phases.
You will learn how to control a budget and schedule and lead a project
team through to successful completion. You will find out how to
anticipate problems and plan for them during the various project phases.

1

And you will discover methods for establishing clear objectives for your project, even when they are not defined at the point of assignment.

Because it's a long-term process, project management causes even well-organized managers to experience difficulty. But if you are accustomed to controlling routine work in your own department, you already understand recurring workload cycles, staffing limitations, and budgetary restraints—the same issues you'll confront with projects.

However, the context is different: First, a project is nonrecurring, so problems and solutions are not matters of routine; second, unlike the limitations on your department's range of tasks, a project often crosses departmental and authority lines; third, a project is planned and organized over several months, whereas recurring tasks are projected ahead only for a few days or weeks.

Managing a project doesn't require any skills you don't already possess; you will employ the same management skills you use elsewhere. The planning, organizing, and execution steps just require greater flexibility and a long-term view than your recurring tasks do, and the project is an exception to the daily or monthly routine.

Running a project is like starting up a new department. What distinguishes both activities from your other tasks is that there's no historical budget, no predictable pattern to the problems or resistance points, and no cycle on which to base today's actions.

Think of this Little Black Book as the foundation of the project structure you'll create. That structure will take on a style, character, and arrangement of its own, but it must rest on a solid base of organizational skills, definition, and control. This book will show you how to take charge of even the most complex project and proceed with confidence in yourself and your project team. But protect this book, and be sure you can trust those who might see you reading it. Keep it locked up in your desk or briefcase, and never leave it out in the open where it may be borrowed permanently. This is your secret project tool; guard it well.

1

Organizing for the Long Term

Every moment spent planning saves three or four in execution.

—Crawford Greenwalt

The newly hired mail room employee noticed an elderly gentle-
man sitting in a corner and slowly sorting interoffice envelopes.
"Who's that?" he asked the supervisor.
"Oh, that's Charley. He's been with the company for about
forty years."
"And he never made it out of the mail room?" the employee
asked.
"He did, but he asked to be transferred here—after spending
several years as a project manager."

Dread. That's a common reaction to being given a project assignment.
Thought of as the corporate version of a root canal, a project is often
seen as something to avoid rather than to seek.

But once you discover that the job of organizing and executing a
project is not all that difficult, the assignment will take on a different
character. Instead of a difficult, if not impossible, task, it will become an
interesting challenge to your organizational skills—perhaps it will serve

3

as an outlet for your creativity or a way to demonstrate your skill—even as an excellent forum for developing your leadership abilities.

The secret is not in learning new skills but in applying the skills you already have, but in a new arena. The project is probaby an exception to your normal routine. You need to operate with an eye to a longer-term deadline than you have in the weekly or monthly cycle you're more likely to experience in your department.

Of course, some managers operate projects routinely, and are accustomed to dealing with a unique set of problems, restrictions, and deadlines in each case. For example, engineers, contractors, or architects move from one project to another, often involving circumstances never encountered before. Still, they apply the same organizational skills to each and every job. That's *their* routine.

It's more likely that you run a department that deals with a series of recurring tasks from one month to another: The same assignments, procedures, and results occur within the cycle; the same people perform the same routines each time; and you can anticipate problems and deal with them in a very predictable way. So when you are given an exceptional task—a project—you may be very uncomfortable and find yourself asking:

> *How do I get started?*
> *Exactly what am I expected to achieve?*
> *Who is responsible for what, and how am I supposed to coordinate the effort?*

It's also likely that you're used to receiving information from a known source and at a specific time. You perform your routines—recording, interpreting, reporting, processing—and then convey the end result to someone else. But on projects, you'll be working with other departments so the steps involved in receiving, performing, and reporting will probably be very different from what you're used to.

This is a big challenge for someone who is assigned a one-time job (or a series of jobs) that are not part of his or her usual experience. And as for all new challenges, the key to staying in control involves the elements of definition, planning, and organization.

PROJECT DEFINITIONS

The definition of *project* varies from one company to another. In some cases, the word is used loosely to describe any task, exceptional or recurring. Thus, a "project" could mean any routine that demands time. In this book, we distinguish between a project and a routine in four ways, as summarized in Figure 1-1.

    1. *A project is an exception.* A project involves investigating, compiling, arranging, and reporting information outside the range of usual activities while routine is defined within the range of a department's function.

Example: The manager of a customer service department prepares monthly reports identifying customer contact trends (complaints, inquiries, suggestions) as part of her routine. When she is given the task of investigating and comparing automated customer service software, she is responsible for a project.

    2. *Project activities are related.* Routines for recurring tasks performed in your department are related to the activities that define and distinguish

Figure 1-1.   Comparing projects and routine.

PROJECT	ROUTINE
Exception to the usual range of functions.	Defined within the scope of the department.
Activites are related.	Routines are related.
Goals and deadlines are specific.	Goals and deadlines are general.
The desired result is identified.	No singular result is identified.

that department only, whereas the activities involved in project phases are related to one another and to a desired end result. So your project may involve coordinating work that not only takes place in your immediate department but extends to actions in other departments, as well as to outside resources.

Example: The customer service manager given the project of investigating automated systems may work with the data processing manager, the marketing department, and several suppliers. Collectively, the internal and external information will help her identify the points of comparison.

3. *Project goals and deadlines are specific.* Recurring tasks may be managed with departmental goals in mind; but these goals tend to remain fixed, or move forward only with time. The same is true of deadlines; you may face weekly or monthly deadlines for completion of reports, processing, and closing. Projects, though, have singular goals that will be either reached or missed. And projects have clear starting points and completion dates.

Example: The customer service manager is told to compare prices and features of software, make a recommendation, and complete a report within three months. This project has a clear goal and deadline. In comparison, her department's routine goals and deadlines extend from one month to another.

4. *The desired result is identified.* Routines are aimed not at one outcome but at maintenance of processes, whereas the research, development of procedures, or construction of systems or buildings on a project produce a tangible, desired result.

Example: For her project, the customer service manager is expected to deliver a conclusive report. It's a one-time assignment, not one that will recur each month. But the routine reports her department generates will still be produced as a maintenance function of her department.

Projects are also distinguished from routines by the way in which they must operate under the three constraints of result, budget, and time (see Figure 1-2). To a degree, all management functions operate within these constraints. For example, your department may be expected to perform and produce certain results; it's subjected to budgeting controls; and its work is planned and executed under a series of deadlines.

Figure 1-2.   Three project constraints.

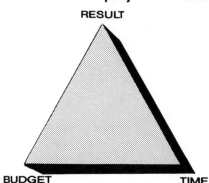

These constraints, while common to all departments and recognized by every manger, are perpetual. Not all three are encountered consistently in all cases. And they might not even serve as guidelines for your actions.

Example: The manager of an insurance claims office keeps an eye on the volume of work, which varies from one day to the next. His primary concern is completion of processing to avoid backlogs of work. That may be called a desired result, but it is a constant one and not a one-time goal.

Example: A department is given an expense budget for the next year. In several cases, assigned expense levels are allocated and beyond the manager's immediate control. Thus, he does not track all aspects of the budget with control in mind.

Example: An accounting department records transactions on a daily basis, and cuts off each day at 3 p.m., when a batch is balanced and processed on an automated system. The daily deadline is part of the recurring routine and has an ongoing series of cut-off points, unlike a longer-term deadline.

But projects succeed or fail purely on the basis of the three constraints; as follows:

1. *Result.* Completion of a specific, defined task or a series of tasks is the primary driving force behind a project. Unlike the recurring tasks faced on the departmental level, a project is targeted to the idea of a finite, one-time result.

2. *Budget.* A project's budget is often separate from the departmental budget. Unlike a department's staff, a project team operates with a degree of independence—in terms of both control and money. Project teams often include people from several different departments; thus, budgetary control cannot be organized along departmental lines. A project may require a capital budget as well as an expense budget. As project manager, you're likely to have a greater degree of control over variances.

3. *Time.* Projects have specific starting points and stopping points. A well-organized project is based on careful controls over completion phases, which involve the use of each team member's time.

DEFINITION AND CONTROL

In later chapters, you'll learn how to manage projects with the constraints of result, budget, and time in mind, constraints that define the project and the way it will be organized. For now, it's important to understand the two components that lead to the successful completion of a project: definition and control. Without either of these, you will be unlikely to achieve (or know) the final result, within the budget, and within the deadline.

Example: A manager is given the assignment of preparing his department for automation. He puts a lot of effort into defining the purpose, breaking out tasks, and devising a schedule and a budget. However, once the work begins, the project falls apart because no control functions were planned. There is no specific assignment of responsibility; nor does the manager compare actual progress to the schedule or watch project expenses to keep them in line with the budget.

Example: A manager embarks on a project with a carefully designed monitoring and control system. She delegates effectively, controls the schedule and budget, and completes the project on time. However, when the final report is presented, she discovers that the result is not what was expected. Why? The manager didn't ask for a clear definition of the purpose at the onset.

As you can see in Figure 1-3, the definition component of a project is broken down into four segments and control into five:

Figure 1-3. Defining and controlling the project.

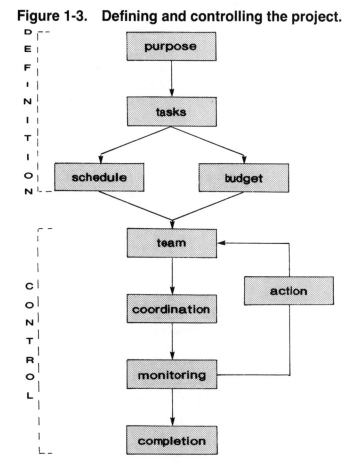

Definition

1. *Purpose.* What is the expectation? Why is the project being undertaken, and what conclusions or answers should it produce?

2. *Tasks.* How can a large project be broken down into a series of short-term progress steps? Remember, although a big project may be overwhelming, smaller portions can be methodically attacked and completed according to a schedule.

3. *Schedule.* What is the final deadline? And with that deadline in mind, how can a series of smaller tasks be arranged, maintained, and scheduled? Proper scheduling of tasks on a week-to-week basis is the key to meeting a long-term deadline.

4. *Budget.* How much should the project cost? Will the company have to invest money in research, capital equipment, promotion, or market testing? What expenses should be planned for, and how much money should be set aside to allow for successful completion?

Control

1. *Team.* As a project manager, you will need to gather the necessary team. You may have to borrow resources from other departments, or use all or part of your own staff. But you can't build the team until you know the purpose, schedule, and budget for the project.

2. *Coordination.* By its very nature, a project demands consistent management. Committees don't work well if they're overly democratic, so as project manager you must be responsible for coordinating the efforts of everyone on the team.

3. *Monitoring.* Your schedule and budget will succeed only if you are able to spot emerging problems and correct them; delegating work to others or creating a control system aren't enough. You also need to track the indicators that tell you whether the project is on schedule and within budget and if the purpose is being achieved at each step along the way.

4. *Action.* If you find that problems are developing, you will need to take action to correct them. If your team is falling behind schedule, you must accelerate the pace of work. If they're exceeding budget, costs and expenses must be brought under control and further variances

eliminated or reduced. This is possible only if you can follow up on discovered problems before they get out of hand.

5. *Completion.* Even if a project is well-managed and kept on schedule for 99 percent of the time period, if that last step isn't taken, the deadline won't be met. Even well-run projects sometimes prove difficult to close out. That final report, the last conclusion, the commitment to paper often prove to be the hardest parts of the entire project.

THE SUCCESSFUL PROJECT MANAGER

A successful project manager knows how to bring together the definition and control elements and operate them efficiently. That means you will need to apply the leadership skills you already apply in running a department and practice the organizational abilities you need to constantly look to the future.

In other words, if you're a qualified department manager, you already possess the skills and attributes for succeeding as a project manager (see Figure 1-4). The criteria by which you will be selected will be similar. Chances are, the project you're assigned will have a direct relationship to the skills you need just to do your job. For example:

- *Organizational and leadership experience.* An executive seeking a qualified project manager usually seeks someone who has already demonstrated the ability to organize work and to lead others. He or she assumes that you will succeed in a complicated long-term project primarily because you have already demonstrated the required skills and experience.

- *Contact with needed resources.* For projects that involve a lot of coordination between departments, divisions, or subsidiaries, top management will look for a project manager who already communicates outside of a single department. If you have the contacts required for a project, it will naturally be assumed that you are suited to run a project across departmental lines.

- *Ability to coordinate a diverse resource pool.* By itself, contact outside of your department may not be enough. You must also be able to work

Figure 1-4. Project manager qualifications.

1. Organizational and leadership experience.

2. Contact with needed resources.

3. Ability to coordinate a diverse resource pool.

4. Communication and procedural skills.

5. Ability to delegate and monitor work.

6. Dependability.

with a variety of people and departments, even when their backgrounds and disciplines are dissimilar. For example, as a capable project manager, you must be able to delegate and monitor work not only in areas familiar to your own department but in areas that are alien to your background.

■ *Communication and procedural skills.* An effective project manager will be able to convey and receive information to and from a number of team members, even when particular points of view are different from his own. For example, a strictly administrative manager should understand the priorities of a sales department, or a customer service manager may need to understand what motivates a production crew.

■ *Ability to delegate and monitor work.* Project managers need to delegate the work that will be performed by each team member, and to monitor that work to stay on schedule and within budget. A contractor who builds a house has to understand the processes involved for work done by each subcontractor, even if the work is highly specialized. The same is true for every project manager. It's not enough merely to assign someone else a task, complete with a schedule and a budget. Delegation and monitoring are effective only if you're also able to supervise and assess progress.

■ *Dependability*. Your dependability can be tested only in one way: by being given responsibility and the chance to come through. Once you gain the reputation as a manager who can and does respond as expected, you're ready to take on a project.

These project management qualifications read like a list of evaluation points for every department manager. If you think of the process of running your department as a project of its own, then you already understand what it's like to organize a project—the difference, of course, being that the project takes place in a finite time period, whereas your departmental tasks are ongoing. Thus, every successful manager should be ready to tackle a project, provided it is related to his or her skills, resources, and experience.

THE METHODICAL MANAGER

To describe someone as methodical may have a negative ring. The distinction is often made between the overly organized, methodical personality and someone who is less structured or more creative. In fact, though, there is no conflict between the two. You can be methodical and creative at the same time.

True creativity demands a methodical, organized approach to problems and is highly structured. Even what appears to be the most unstructured outcome may be the result of tremendous organization and planning. As project manager, you will often need to muster all your creativity to deal with the unexpected problems that come up during the course of a project. And the more methodical your approach to the project, the better your chances of finding creative and appropriate solutions.

The methodical project manager knows the right questions to ask. At the time a project is assigned, your checklist should include the seven questions (listed in Figure 1-5) that will lead to complete definition. These are:

Figure 1-5. Checklist: questions to ask.

1. What is the purpose of this project?

2. What will the outcome look like?

3. What problems will be encountered and solved?

4. What is my responsibility?

5. What is my authority?

6. What is my budget?

7. What is the deadline?

1. *What is the purpose of this project?* From the description of an assignment you may make a series of assumptions about what the person making the assignment wants. But in fact, he or she might have something completely different in mind. A large number of the communication problems you confront involve definition.

Example: As manager of the accounting department, you are given the project of developing a procedures manual for preparing budgets. At first, it seems obvious that the purpose is to define expense budgeting. But with a little more discussion, you learn that the desired budget is intended not for general expenses but for capital assets. The procedures will be much different based on this definition.

2. *What will the outcome look like?* Be sure you know exactly what someone else expects to see at the end of the project. If you're given the role of designing a series of procedures for the company, does that mean you will write an entire manual, or will you just provide guidelines for each department? Will your project require a written report, and if so, how much detail should be included? Will you be expected to make a presentation, and if so, in what format?

3. *What problems will be encountered and solved?* Always assume that a project will identify and solve a series of specific problems. You can't expect someone else to list all of the possible issues that will come up; in fact, the project process may itself be designed to define the problems rather than to overcome them. Even when you suspect that a range of problems will be discovered beyong the initial discussion, a project begins with an assumption: A specific problem or series of problems is identified, and your purpose is to solve them or suggest alternatives. Define your project in these terms. Ask, What problems will this project solve? If you have not gotten a clear answer, don't proceed until the issues have been discussed and clarified for you.

4. *What is my responsibility?* As project manager you deserve a clear definition of what you're expected to do. Will you be responsible for identifying solutions? For putting them into effect? Or only for suggesting alternatives?

Be sure you know how far you're expected to go. Find out what level of responsibility you're being given and where the limitations are. In some cases, you may be asked to put changes into action, but only to the extent that they'll affect one division, subsidiary, or department.

5. *What is my authority?* Authority should be defined as carefully as responsibility. If you're given the authority to recruit team members from other departments, change procedures, or make a final decision, that should be made clear. And the limits on authority should also be explained.

Example: A manager met with the company president, who gave him the assignment of reorganizing the location of departments on one floor. Several departments were spread out in different areas, and some had too little or too much floor space. The manager understood the assignment to mean actually putting changes into effect. But when he informed other managers of the pending change, much of the reaction was negative. The project manager met with the president again, surprised that no one knew about his assumed mandate. "I only wanted you to make a recommendation," the president said, "not to start moving desks and chairs."

In this case, the manager was given what he thought was a specific assignment. But without establishing his level of authority, he ran into problems and did more than what the president had in mind. Regardless of who fails to communicate, assume it's your job to find out how much authority you'll have as project manager.

6. *What is my budget?* Some projects can be executed with little expense beyond the commitment of time. Others involve spending money on research, writing reports, or purchasing equipment.

Always begin your project with a clear understanding of the budget. Don't overlook the expense of employee time, since that defines the real cost to the company of achieving the desired result.

7. *What is the deadline?* Always ask for a specific deadline. Only with a deadline will it be possible to set a schedule and budget for successful completion. But while not having a deadline is a potential problem, it's more likely that assigned projects will place a strain on your resources. If you believe a deadline is too short, ask for more time. If it isn't granted, you'll just have to put your organizational skills to work and coordinate the phases of the project to meet it.

In establishing a schedule, you can often overlap some phases to make more efficient use of time. And it's always smart to allow a little more time than you'll actually need to build a buffer into your schedule. But you may find yourself running a project without any time luxury at all.

CLASSIFYING THE PROJECT

How you approach, plan, and organize a project will depend on its nature. If the routines in your department are, in fact, more like projects than recurring tasks, you can use the project management approach to organizing many of the tasks you execute.

Example: A research department manager applies project management techniques for every assignment, altering the recurring task to suit the complexity and scope of research to be performed.

Example: The production editor in a publishing company plans the editing, design, and printing of each book based on publication deadline, delivery time, length of the manuscript, and budget.

Example: A construction company estimator organizes each project bid based on the type of job and approximate complexity of the task.

While the steps involved in defining, controlling, and finalizing a project may be the same, the degree of effort will vary depending on the project. Compare the different emphases for these projects:

Test Marketing a New Project:	The method of market testing may be well understood, so the project emphasis will be in two areas: (1) selecting a representative test region and (2) evaluating results accurately.
Installing a New Automated System:	Here, the definition phase is all-important. You may need to determine exactly what automation requirements each phase of operations needs; in some instances, the project itself will be designed just to identify those routines that should be automated.
Changing Departmental Procedures:	You might have flexibility in the deadline, especially if you originate the project on your own. However, a specific deadline should still be imposed so that your project team completes its work within a finite time frame.

Projects, whether part of the usual work in your department or assigned as one-time jobs, can be classified and organized according to the scope and complexity of the work. Classification can be made based on:

- The number of resources you will use outside of your immediate department
- The size of the required project team
- The time span between inception and deadline
- Your familiarity with the information

As project manager, you will stay on schedule and within budget and complete the job on time by defining and organizing carefully. In later chapters, we will demonstrate the methods for mastering even the most complicated project. No job is too large if it's first defined completely and then broken down into logical and progressive steps. Chapter 2 examines the initial phase: creating the plan and defining objectives.

WORK PROJECT

1. Explain the distinction between projects and routines according to the following:
   a. Range of functions
   b. Relationship of activities or routines
   c. Goals and deadlines
   d. Project results
2. What are the three constraints under which a project is executed? How do these constraints define your control responsibility?
3. Compare the definition and control elements of a project. Why are both essential to successful execution of the assignment?

2

Creating the Plan

You read a book from the beginning to the end. You run a business in the opposite way. You start with the end, and then you do everything you must to reach it.

—Harold Geneen

"Planning is the key," the project manager explained to her assistant as their lunch came to an end. "I invited you here today to emphasize that point. As part of this team, I expect you to understand the importance of planning ahead."

She stopped as the waiter approached, and accepted the tab. She looked at the total for a moment, and then quietly asked her assistant, "Can you lend me twenty dollars?"

All successful projects begin with a clear definition of the end result. That is, you need to identify the purpose and structure of the job, what it will look like upon completion, the problems that will be solved, and the objectives you'll meet as project manager. So before you actually start work on any project, be sure that these questions are answered:

1. *Exactly what objectives am I expected to meet?* Has the project been defined well enough so that you know what the assignment is? By identifying objectives, you can better define the end result.
2. *Who is the project for?* Another way to define the end result is by making sure you know who will use the project results, and for what purpose.

19

3. *What problems will be solved by the end result?* Coming up with a new procedure or new information may be the tangible result of the project; but to make that end result worthwhile, you will need to know what current or past problems should be solved by the efforts put into your project.

This chapter explains the methods for defining your project task: building your resource network, the purpose of the first project meeting, setting objectives, coming up with an initial schedule, and identifying the key elements of information, budgets, and team commitment.

SETTING LEADERSHIP GOALS

After you come up with a clear definition, schedule, and budget for your project, you need to plan for the way in which you'll lead your project team. Because projects are often seen by team members as intrusions into their routines—extra work that's imposed on them—you may have to contend with resistance within the team, or at least help team members resolve scheduling conflicts.

To make a project work smoothly, you may have to alter your leadership style. You should also clearly define your function and the function of the team.

Some suggestions are listed in Figure 2-1 and explained as follows:

1. *Clarify your leadership role.* A department manager may gain the respect of his or her department staff over time, regardless of individual style. But a project manager, like each person on the team, is often thrust into a temporary leadership role, often over individuals from other departments. In this situation, it's important to let your project team know how you perceive that role.

Your function will vary depending on the complexity of each project and on the size and nature of the team. But for most projects, you will function not as a supervisor or mediator but as a coordinator. You may often have to participate directly in many phases of the job to make sure that resources work together, budgets are controlled, and schedules are met.

Figure 2-1.   Project leadership goals.

1. Clarify your leadership role.

2. Follow through on all aspects of the job.

3. Emphasize organization and scheduling.

4. Be aware of team priorities and conflicts.

5. Be available to team members.

6. Ask for participation and respond to it.

7. Always remember the end result.

2. Follow through on all aspects of the job. Remember that because projects are exceptions, team members may not understand their roles as clearly as you'd like or might assume. So you must be able to follow through on assignments and make sure they're clearly understood in terms of the desired result and deadline—a level of follow-through greater than you'd need in supervising a seasoned department. A good method is to approach assignments and supervision as though you were training new employees—at the same time not becoming so involved in overseeing that the team members feel like trainees.

3. Emphasize organization and scheduling. Project leaders depend on a very well organized schedule of work and division of assignments. Therefore, it's important to write everything down. Use checklists to make sure that work is proceeding on schedule and that everyone knows what's expected of them and when completion is due. You may want to work from a clipboard and solve problems as they come up, even to the point that you don't get directly involved in the work itself.

4. *Be aware of team priorities and conflicts.* Rarely do project team members abandon their own recurring tasks to spend all of their time on temporary projects. Your project is more likely to represent extra duty; some team members may even consider it a low priority. They are likely to face conflicts in deadlines, since departmental tasks and project tasks cannot both be completed within a limited amount of time. This problem is especially difficult to resolve when team members report to you for the project and to someone else the rest of the time.

Therefore, ask team members to let you know in advance about future scheduling conflicts, and then seek a solution—if necessary, by reassigning tasks. To avoid unnecessary conflicts that place team members in the middle, stay in touch with the managers of their departments.

5. *Be available to team members.* Just as your team members must continue to execute departmental tasks, you will have to continue leading your department. But no matter how much pressure you're under, and no matter how much work you have, you should be available to your team. When they approach you with problems or questions, be sure you make time to work out a solution.

6. *Ask for participation and respond to it.* A team functions more democratically than a department; otherwise it isn't really a team. Ask your team to offer ideas, propose solutions and procedures, and take part in executing the project's objective. Most of all, make their participation a reality, not just a concept. You need to listen well when members offer ideas; when the ideas make sense, be willing to change your assumptions.

7. *Always remember the end result.* When you're busy solving scheduling and budget problems and overcoming delays in getting information, it's easy to lose sight of your project objective. Remind yourself constantly of what you want to achieve, and guide your decisions and actions by the end result.

BUILDING YOUR RESOURCE NETWORK

Project managers organize and plan by identifying and then building a network. This network consists of people from their departments, other departments, and, in some instances, outside of the company.

Example: A sales department manager was assigned the project of developing procedures for salespeople, to ensure follow-through with customers. Salespeople were not delivering orders correctly or supplying important information needed to fulfill their orders. The manager was told to come up with a sales manual, as well as newly designed order forms, and to ensure that the fulfillment department would be able to deliver what the customers wanted.

The project manager made a list of the people who would be needed to fulfill his objective. They included:

- *Salespeople,* who were familiar with the order completion process and who knew the kinds of problems that had come up in the past. Their participation would help in the design of practical procedures and forms that could be put into use and that would also resolve the problems that were creating poor fulfillment.

- *The manager of the fulfillment department,* who was aware of the same problems, but from a different point of view. He would be able to list the information needed to do his job and suggest how it should be arranged on a form. He would also be able to recommend follow-up procedures.

- *An employee in the customer service department,* who had recently completed a report summarizing the types of complaints received from customers. This employee was aware of the types of errors customers reported, which mainly had to do with delays, shipment of the wrong products, and incomplete orders.

- *An outside resource,* for designing, typesetting, and printing forms.

In addition, the project manager assigned two employees from his department to help with the task of compiling information from others and designing preliminary forms, writing new procedures, and following up on approval and suggestions from other departments. One of the most important functions of this project was to come up with one form and one procedure that would satisfy the requirements of both the salespeople and the fulfillment department.

Having the right people on your project team is essential, whether they play an active role or an advisory one. You can often coordinate and execute a project by combining a fairly small team with an extensive advisory network. Making this distinction helps you execute the management task, because you will isolate a relatively small core of direct team members and use advisers only to solve specific problems that will come up in a few project phases.

Example: A sales manager had two of his own employees on his team, but he also asked for help from salespeople, fulfillment, and customer service to develop information necessary to the project.

Depending on the complexity of the project and the number of people on the team, you may structure the project one of two ways: direct structure or organizational structure. A direct structure is one in which you are in touch with each team member, and it is used when there's no need for a middle reporting layer. This structure is similar to that of a small department in which the manager supervises each employee. This approach has the advantage of simplicity, direct contact, and lack of the bureaucracy that might be created with middle reporting layers. The direct team structure is illustrated in Figure 2-2.

The organizational structure is necessary if your project team includes many internal and external members and when your monitoring

Figure 2-2.   Direct team structure.

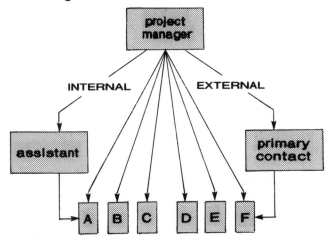

and control functions will take up most of your time. In this case, you need to be able to delegate supervision and scheduling control to an internal assistant *and* to an external primary contact. You will still want to be in touch with members of the team, and it will be important to avoid setting up an overly bureaucratic system; that would only take away from the desired effectiveness of your team. The purpose of the organizational structure is to share responsibility for a larger group, illustrated in Figure 2-3.

The structure you choose to build for your project team depends on the scope and complexity of each project. You want to create an effective team that's able to operate with the appropriate level of supervision and without unnecessary reporting layers. Team members need to communicate with leadership, whether that means you alone or assistants to whom you have delegated clear responsibilities.

Example: One manager is currently responsible for two different projects. The first project is short-term and fairly simple, involving a team of three employees. For this project, she has put a direct team structure in place. The second project is more complicated, both in objective and

Figure 2-3. Organizational team structure.

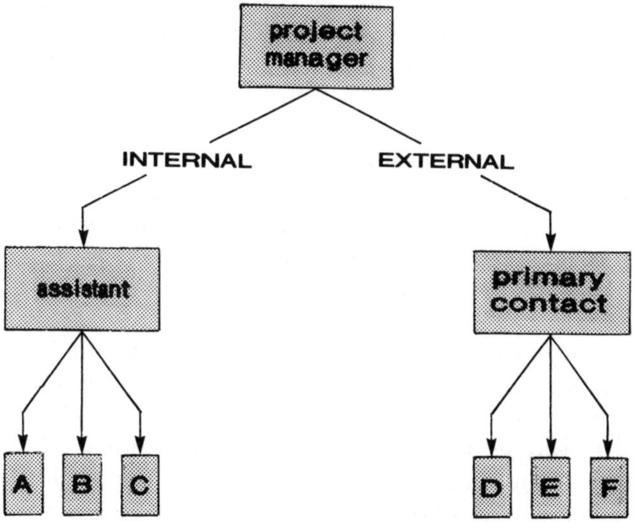

size of the team. She has appointed an assistant to coordinate the work of internal team members, and also depends on a fellow manager as a primary contact for project team members in that manager's department.

THE PROJECT ANNOUNCEMENT MEETING

Getting your project off to a healthy, well-defined start depends on your approach: how you lead, how you seek definition, and the initial organization of the team, schedule, and budget. But it's also necessary to communicate your purpose and approach to your team. Thus, a project announcement meeting is essential.

Do you really need an announcement meeting? It may be possible to set the tone and define your purpose without gathering people together; but a preliminary meeting can save a lot of time and effort later, and can help avoid misunderstandings about authority levels and the nature of the assignment.

Example: An accounting manager was assigned the project of setting priorities for automation. The task included interviewing the heads of each department and recommending routines that should be given priority. But the department managers were not advised of the project. The accountant found these managers to be defensive and suspicious; they weren't sure whose idea the project was, the accountant's or top management's. A great deal of effort went into explanation, and the project proved difficult to complete.

This project could have been executed more efficiently if an initial meeting had been called. The accountant and each department manager should have been invited, as well as the executive who made the assignment.

If an announcement meeting is not called at the time a project is assigned to you, recommend calling one. The executive should briefly explain the purpose and objective of the task and clearly identify you as the project manager. Once everyone understands what you'll be doing, it will be easier for you to organize your project team and contact the resources you'll need. Most of all, a brief meeting will help avoid your having to explain what you're doing and why, or having to deal tactfully with other managers who have not been informed about your project.

Support your recommendation for the announcement meeting with these points:

1. Announcing a new project defines it for everyone involved, and clarifies the intended purpose. If the meeting is not held, definition will be a problem each time you have to contact a resource.
2. The meeting helps ensure success, because everyone gets the message at the same time and from the same authoritative source. Your ability to lead the project team is aided when the project is launched from the top.
3. A demonstration of executive support for the project manager helps the team to achieve its goals. However, it's important to let others in on the decision when they or employees reporting to them will also be affected, either as a team member or as a resource for the team.

If you have identified your project team by the time the announcement meeting takes place, each member should be invited along with individual managers or supervisors of their departments. Introducing the project to everyone—team members and their supervisors—makes your job of working with other departments much easier.

There's a significant difference between trying to achieve a project task that conflicts with departmental goals and working *with* other managers to resolve problems. Inviting the managers to the initial project meeting makes them feel included in the process. That sets a positive tone and helps you to function as project manager. The alternative is having to continually struggle with a manager who was left out of the decision-making process at the beginning.

SETTING PROJECT OBJECTIVES

Once your project is launched, how do you get the team working together? It won't be enough to explain what the project will achieve and begin handing out assigments. Your team should be oriented with as much information as possible. And their participation should be encouraged from the beginning.

After the announcement meeting, plan your first team meeting. But remember, meetings should be limited in frequency and time. You can't get anything done if you and your team spend all of your time meeting and discussing the project. After the initial team meeting, plan to get together only a few more times—to review progress, resolve any special problems that have come up, and ensure that the schedule and budget are on track.

The initial team meeting should be designed to help team members identify their contribution to the task. Try these ideas shown in Figure 2-4 to help your team:

1. *List the problems the team will solve.* Start with your own list, then ask members to add any other problems they're aware of. Different points of view will help you define the objectives of the project and will increase the value of the final result.

2. *Offer solutions the team should achieve.* List solutions to each of the

Figure 2-4.   Agenda: initial project meeting.

1. List the problems the team will solve.

2. Offer solutions the team should achieve.

3. Describe information the team will need.

4. Propose initial assignments.

5. Plan the entire project in advance.

problems you've listed, then ask the team to offer alternative ideas. At this point in the plan, you will want to define the team's approach as thoroughly as possible so that no one is left out of the process.

3. *Describe information the team will need.* Write out the information as well as the sources for research, historical facts, and financial data you will need. Then ask the team to suggest other methods for improving on the process or to identify resources for the raw data you'll need.

4. *Propose initial assignments.* Identify task areas and suggest which team members you think are best-suited to take responsibility for them. But don't finalize anything at this point. Remember, this is an intitial planning and brainstorming meeting. Let team members define their own roles as much as possible. If people sense that they are involved in deciding how the project will proceed, they will be more participative as a group.

5. *Plan the entire project in advance.* Establish a preliminary division of responsibility. This gives the team an idea of the scope of the entire job. Later, when you put together your schedule and budget, you may want to modify this initial decision in consultation with the team, in consideration of any schedule conflicts, and to ensure a fair division of work load.

THE INITIAL SCHEDULE

Besides establishing a preliminary division of responsibilities, start your project by coming up with a schedule for completion (see Figure 2-5)— not only of the entire project, but of each phase. Begin with two dates: the start date and the completion date. In between, you need to identify logical phases (including responsibilites among your team) and a realistic deadline for each.

Some phases may overlap. When two or more team members are working independently, it will not always be necessary for one group to wait for the other. Overlapping of phases adds a lot of flexibility to a schedule that otherwise would leave little room for delayed completion.

Your initial schedule should include the following deadlines:

- Definition of purpose and identification of specific task responsibilities, scheduling, and budget
- Identification of phases
- Review of completed phases
- Completion (e.g., preparation of reports, final versions of documentation, forms, and other results of the project)

Figure 2-5.   Initial schedule.

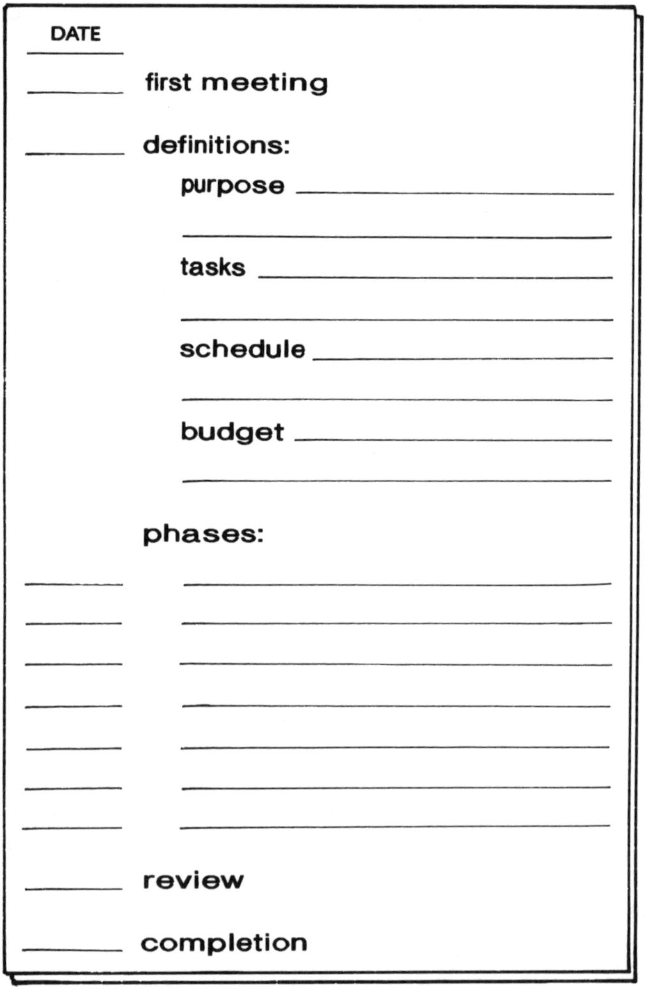

This first step must be preliminary, and as project leader, you need to maintain a degree of flexibility. As your team begins to understand the scope of the project they will be in a better position to define the best level of participation, to share scheduling and phasing ideas with you, and to coordinate your project needs according to their own departmental time constraints and deadlines.

Once your team has been exposed to the scope of the project, you will be responsible for developing a final listing of phase and task assignments, developing the actual project schedule, identifying information sources and types, and coming up with a budget. These requirements will be more complete if you first give the team the opportunity to make suggestions and propose alternative processes.

IDENTIFYING KEY ELEMENTS

If you start your project with an announcement meeting and follow that by holding an initial project team meeting, you should have a fairly well defined task ahead of you. Now you need to identify the elements that will allow you to achieve clearly stated project goals. These include information, a budget, and details of project team commitments.

Information

The first element is information resources. Raw data or other reports may have to be gathered from other departments or outside sources; if this information doesn't already exist or is not available to you and your team members, you may need to research and develop data of your own.

Analyze information needs by answering these questions:

1. *What sources can supply available information, and what information must be developed by the project team?* If information already exists, identify and make use of it. There's no point in duplicating what someone else has already done.
2. *How will we verify information?* Be aware that someone else's information may be out of date, inaccurate, or subject to misinterpretation. If your conclusions will be based on information supplied by someone else, plan to verify it.

3. *How much time will it take to get information from an outside source?* Be sure to include enough time in your schedule for an outside source to gather and send information to you.

4. *How much time will it take to study or arrange the information we receive or develop?* Translating raw data into meaningful information may represent a major time commitment; that too must be built into your project schedule.

Budget

Your project budget should be planned with staffing and information sources in mind. Will you need to purchase or lease equipment? Pay for outside information? Travel? Have you allowed for the expense of developing and printing the final report? If you will have to include illustrative material such as forms, charts or graphs, flowcharts, or training aids, budget for the costs of design and drafting.

You will achieve maximum control by preparing a budget on a phase-by-phase basis. In that way, you will be able to monitor actual versus budget as the project proceeds. Without this added feature, you cannot control overall expenses of the project or quickly identify areas where overruns are occurring.

Also plan for the method of review. Will you break down each phase and prepare a report comparing actual to budget? Will you delegate budget review? And what steps will you, as project manager, take to reverse negative trends discovered in the review process?

Team Commitment

The degree of motivation among your team members will determine how well the entire project proceeds. By leadership example you can maintain a sense of participation and commitment. But be aware of these factors:

- *Day-to-day commitments.* Team members must be able to continue with their ongoing departmental responsibilities as well as respond to project demands.

■ *Priorities.* If team members think of projects as impositions on their schedules, it will be very difficult to inspire and lead them. Preliminary planning, responsibility assignments, and participative style you encourage can help alleviate this problem.

■ *Coordination.* If you are able to demonstrate through organizational ability and preplanning that you can help team members work well together, they will be more likely to respond positively. But if they feel that the process is poorly defined, the objectives are not spelled out, or that procedures are inefficient, you cannot expect a coordinated effort.

■ *Leadership Support.* As project manager you are responsibile for coordinating your team's efforts and for staying on schedule and within budget. But beyond that, to succeed in working with your team, you must provide all needed support. That means working directly with team members to solve problems, overcome resistance from outside sources, and avoid scheduling conflicts.

Your project will work best when you invest energy and time planning—before the project work begins. Teams function well when the leader defines and organizes the task ahead and when the end result is clearly explained and agreed upon. This is possible only when you choose the best possible team for a specific project. Chapter 3 explains how to choose your team and identify areas of responsibility.

WORK PROJECT

1. Describe a project appropriate for use of the direct team structure, and explain the advantages of this approach.
2. What types of projects will be better operated using the organization team structure? Compare this structure to the direct team structure.
3. List three topics that should be included on the agenda of the initial project meeting.

3

Choosing the Project Team

The hammers must be swung in cadence, when more than one is hammering the iron.

—Giordano Bruno

"I don't think I'm going to have a good time working on this project," an employee told a friend. *"We just finished up our first meeting, and the manager talked the whole time about teamwork."*

"Then why are you so worried?" the friend asked.

"It wasn't what he said that bothered me so much," the first one answered, *"but those steel marbles he kept playing with the whole time."*

The people on a team ultimately determine whether or not a project succeeds. Whether a troop of boy scouts or the crew of an aircraft carrier, everyone on the team has to be able to agree on goals before they can work together.

The larger your team and the greater its diversity, the more complicated your task as project managers. A team with only two members—one leader and one follower—involves a singular line of communication. But when a team consists of people from many departments, chances increase that conflicts in goals, communication, and motives will arise to complicate your life.

THE IMPOSED TEAM PROBLEM

As the theory goes, a project manager is selected for a job and then allowed to gather a team of his or her own choosing. But in practice, teams are often chosen without consulting the manager.

You may find out you already have a team when you receive your assignment. Perhaps the executive giving you the job assumes that the team should be chosen by someone at his or her level. The motive may be a worthwhile one. For example, since team members are usually drawn from a number of departments, the vice president giving you the job may believe it will be easier for you to get cooperation from other managers when all assignments come from the top. But an imposed team poses a number of problems for you as project manager.

If you are given an assignment *and* team members, without the opportunity to become involved in the selection, you are starting out at a clear disadvantage. Unfortunately, you might find yourself in this situation for one or more projects. For example, when a vice president names you as leader and assigns several people from a number of departments to work with you, there is no guarantee that the team will be the right one for the job or that the team members' managers will be pleased with the decision.

In some cases, a team is composed, not of the most capable people in the organization, but of the most available. Employees whose work is highly valued may be so much in demand that they simply aren't available, to you or to anyone else except their department manager. So by elimination, the imposed team could consist of the least capable people or of those who have not yet proved valuable as team players.

To solve the problems of having a team imposed on you, consider the idea shown in Figure 3-1 and explained here:

1. *Suggest a different approach.* Simply complaining about the way project teams are put together in your organization may not lead to a better idea. It's much more effective to offer a solution that makes sense

Figure 3-1.   Guidelines: imposed teams.

1. Suggest a different approach.

2. Do your best with what you are given.

3. Give team members the chance to excel.

4. Request team members who work out well.

5. Ask to take part in the selection process.

6. Suggest that department managers should be involved as well.

to top management. If they recognize the value of allowing project managers to choose their own teams, they will be more likely to allow you to take part in team selection.

2. *Do your best with what you are given.* Even after suggesting a more sensible approach, you may still end up with an imposed team. But you still have the assignment. Do your best to achieve your project goals, even if your team is incomplete. You may later be able to make your best argument to management based on a track record of past projects; it will be better for all concerned if you are able to complete a project to expectations, even with a team you did not choose.

3. *Give team members the chance to excel.* Just because a team is imposed does not always mean its members are incapable of performing well. Give each team member the chance to do his or her best work; you may be very pleased with the results. In some cases, an employee whose

performance has been substandard or untried may be waiting for the opportunity you can offer through the project.

4. *Request team members who work out well.* Learn from your own experience. If a team member has already performed well on one of your projects, request him or her for your current project. Even if your boss doesn't go along with the idea of allowing you to pick your own team, you still may be able to influence the team selection somewhat by stating your preferences.

5. *Ask to take part in the selection process.* You may not have the absolute right to choose your own team, but you can ask to be at least involved in making the selection. Since you are the one who will be expected to complete the project successfully, you should make this point: The team itself is critical to the project; therefore, you, as project manager, should be included in the selection process.

6. *Suggest that department managers be involved as well.* There are other managers who should be brought in and consulted when a team is selected: the managers of each team member's department. You can make a number of good arguments for this idea: First, the managers will have to get by with less help for the amount of time you'll need to use their employees; second, they are in the best position to know who is qualified to help you with your project; third, involving them at the start paves the way for a better working relationship between you and them. If each manager is consulted beforehand, even only as a courtesy, your job will be that much easier.

In a more enlightened business environment, management will give you a project assignment and then ask you to put together a team. But you may still have certain restricitons. For example, you probably won't be allowed to recruit anyone you want from any department. It's more likely that you will be free to use people from your own department and also to request help from others—but subject to approval both from the top and from the managers of the other departments.

THE COMMITMENT PROBLEM

Even when a clear schedule is prepared and carefully controlled, a budget is monitored and used to avoid overspending, and precise project goals are defined, a project may still lack an organized structure.

Some people feel only that a certain number of bodies are needed to execute the tasks necessary to complete the job. According to this theory, it doesn't really matter *who* the people are. It only matters that they are able to follow orders and have the time to give to the project. This theory is based on the idea that time and labor are absolute and that individual skills are of secondary importance.

The problem, though, is that some randomly selected team members, even if directly involved in the work connected to your project, may not belong on your team for one or more of the following reasons:

- They don't work well with you.
- They don't work well with the rest of your team.
- They don't have the time to commit to your project.
- Their department managers don't want to give up their labor for the time you'll need.
- They have no commitment to the project or to its goals.

These issues should be addressed at the time the suggestion is made to include someone on your team. Otherwise, they will become only too apparent once the project is launched and problems begin to surface.

Your ideal team member should be committed to the project and able to put in the time and the energy to make it succeed. Commitment is not limited to having the hours available. A valuable team member understands the desired end result and is willing to work with you to make it happen. If that commitment isn't there, you will be struggling with the individual throughout the time you're involved with the project.

A team member who is told to take part in your project may sense that it is *your* chance to succeed, not the team member's. Thus, he or she may have no actual commitment, or even a reason to make one. If the assignment is truly temporary, what is the team member's motivation for making it work?

You may run into this problem more than once. If your team members believe they are anonymous bodies, thrown together to help you succeed without recognition for their work, they won't be committed to the job. And because the project will be viewed as temporary extra work, they can't see how it will help their careers.

These are not just negative attitudes. They're very human. Why should people work hard to make a project succeed when their perception is that it's for someone else's benefit and that someone else will receive recognition for their work?

Therefore, you need to identify the specific features that will give your team members the personal interest and motivation to focus their energy on the project. A team is created not by assigning someone a job but by action and opportunity. Action goes beyond stating that a team exists and expecting it to be true; you need to give the team a chance to act like a team. And that means giving individuals the chance to take charge of their parts in the project. You must supervise, of course, but allow others to apply their skills and creativity. The question you need to ask when pulling together a team is, "How can I inspire the individuals working on this project so that they will *want* it to succeed?"

AREAS OF RESPONSIBILITY

Successful teams strike a balance between two conflicting attributes: individual initiative and group needs. On the one hand, each individual wants to believe that he or she has an opportunity to make decisions— the authority to apply his or her talents in coming up with solutions. On the other hand, the larger goal of the project rules, and each individual must work with the others as a single team.

How can you achieve a compromise between the desire to satisfy an individual ego and the less personal team priority? The answer is to identify areas of responsibility rather than merely pass out tasks.

Building a team is very difficult when you are the sole authority for assigning jobs to the bodies on your team. An alternative is to break down the project and its phases into distinct assignment ranges and then give each team member the responsibility for executing one or more of those ranges.

Example: A project manager in a marketing research company had always experienced difficulty in getting team members to work together. So when a new project was assigned to produce a public survey, he took a different approach. Instead of listing phases and then passing out tasks to team members, he began by identifying experienced and dependable team members. He then matched responsibilities to each individual.

Every phase of the project was scheduled on the basis of responsibility ranges (with listings of tasks within that range). Team members assigned a range were given great freedom to accomplish their particular roles in each phase in terms of working with other team members, meeting deadlines, and solving problems in their own way.

A critical point concerning this approach: As project manager, you must set boundaries on the range of tasks and also ensure that there is a complete understanding of task goals. For example, a project team member who is assigned the job of interpreting market test data will need you to tell him what tests to apply and to check conclusions with you before simply incorporating them into the final report.

As project manager, you must stay in touch with the team, both to supervise when necessary and to be available if problems do arise. But once the team, schedule, and budget have been completed, *your* primary area of responsibility is to make sure the job gets done.

The area of responsibility approach is satisfying for the individuals on the team. It provides the incentive they need to make their best effort. It also expresses your confidence in them, an action that often brings out everyone's best. When team members have a sense of direct control, they are most likely to provide you with their best efforts.

Example: A company's treasurer assigned a manager the project of completely revising the financial reports issued for the company each month. He explained the shortcomings of the reports, and left it to the manager to select a team, work with the data processing department, and achieve results. The final results were due in six months.

The manager chose two people from her own department to work on the project. She also asked a programmer from data processing to join her team. They met, discussed the project, and decided upon a schedule and deadlines. Then the manager assigned her two employees specific responsibilities. One was asked to design reports that would meet the treasurer's criteria. The other was asked to define file requirements and changes in input. The two were to meet periodically with the programmer to discuss program changes.

The manager's area of responsibility was to ensure that each employee's goals were being met and that each phase was being completed on schedule. Using this method, she completed the project on time and to everyone's satisfaction.

In this case, the project manager had been given the freedom to organize the project as she chose. She passed along this approach by selecting the right team members and then giving them areas of responsibility—and the freedom to perform their tasks. The project manager was very involved, but only to the extent needed by the team members to do their jobs. In a sense, she coordinated a series of smaller projects between her team members—passing along the trust and confidence the treasurer had given her.

ESTIMATING TIME REQUIREMENTS

Project managers often run into problems because they try to assign tasks rather than areas of responsibility. In the belief that a highly structured, organized form of management is the only key to project success, they may overlook the need of team members to be given a share of the job, instead of just being told what to do.

Scheduling and the giving out of assignments cannot be separated from one another. They are part of the same process of defining areas of responsibility. The person who is given responsibility for a range of duties may be told what to do; or he or she can be given the defined end result and then left alone to achieve it.

You might give a team member the actual responsibility for one complete phase of a project. But it's more likely that you will coordinate the phase, while identifying the functions he or she will fulfill. The method you use to estimate time requirements will also define how completely you allow each team member to execute his or her part of the job.

Example: One project manager broke down each phase according to the tasks involved. She then met with her team and passed out the schedule, commenting, "This is your list of tasks. You have one week to complete each one."

Example: Another project manager took a different approach to the time estimate. He first prepared a list of each task within a phase and then estimated the time he thought it would take. He met with the team and asked everyone to provide their own estimate of time requirements. Whenever a conflict arose, the entire team compared estimates and discussed them. The purpose of this exercise was to identify potential weak links in the schedule and then to plan for them. Ultimately, the project manager allowed each team member to determine his or her own estimate within a phase. The only estimate he imposed on the team member was to complete the phase while adhering to the deadline for the entire project.

For some projects the area of responsibility dictates not only tasks but responsibility for an entire phase. For others, one phase will encompass work for several, even for all, of the members. In either event, the issues of time and responsibility should be discussed with the team. Your role will be to ensure timely completion of phases and conformity to the budget. Allow team members to run their areas of responsibility (or phases) in their own way, even if that means one individual delegating to another.

WORKING WITH OUTSIDE DEPARTMENTS

One of the issues that will present conflicts for your project will be the priorities of the team members' own departments. You may need to adjust your schedule to allow for these recurring tasks and priorities.

We all have a tendency to believe what we're working on today is of the highest possible priority. This causes conflicts, because others may have the same attitude. But when you, as project manager, come into conflict with a department manager over priorities, always assume that his or her department comes first. There are three reasons for this:

1. *You need the other manager's support.* No matter how the employee ended up on your time—voluntarily, by imposition, or by agreement of the department manager—remember that your success depends on the cooperation of others. In a sense, the other manager is part of your project team, even if he or she provides no more than support.

2. *A department's work is permanent while your project is temporary.* Keep your project in perspective. Employees who must function on your team also have to continue to function in their own departments—meaning that their evaluations will be performed by their managers and that they will be expected to execute departmental duties no matter how urgently your work has to get done.

3. *Departmental tasks recur and often are tied to deadlines.* You have immediate phase deadlines and an overall deadline, both of which may be critical. But in addition to pressure to complete work in their areas of responsibility for your project, team members also have recurring tasks in their departments. When setting your schedule, be aware of the potential problems this may create. Try to anticipate the workloads that team members will face, e.g., at the close of a monthly cycle, and arrange your own deadlines with those departmental workloads in mind.

When conflicts of any nature arise, your first step should be to meet with each department manager to seek a solution that will satisfy everyone. Avoid placing the team member in the middle between two demanding managers, each concerned with a conflicting deadline.

The purpose of your meeting is to resolve conflicts so that they won't recur. Make your position clear: You are meeting because you respect the work of the department, you understand the priority of work, and you want to help. Communicating your desire to work *with* the manager and not *against* the goals of his or her department will enlist much more cooperation.

Example: One project manager was under a great deal of pressure to complete the last phase of a project. He was already behind schedule, and his boss was applying pressure to finish it up. But two of his team members could not complete essential tasks due to deadlines within their own departments. The project manager tried to explain his deadline problems to their department manager, and insisted that the team members be freed to work on the project first—to no avail.

Example: Another project manager realized that it would be very difficult to complete her project on time because of another department's deadline. She met with the other manager and explained the problem. Together, they came up with a solution that involved recruiting addi-

tional help from still another department to relieve deadline pressure for
two project team members.

THE EXECUTIVE POINT OF VIEW

You might be surprised to discover the point of view held by the person
who assigned the project to you. In some cases, executives are supportive; in others they are surprised that you can't solve all problems on
your own. Some executives assume that a capable project manager never
has to ask for help and that you are competent enough to handle all
problems without involving someone else.

Given the uncertain nature of some projects and the cultural status
in many companies, such points of view may be unrealistic. Nevertheless,
some executives do prefer to assign a project and then walk away from
it—at least until the deadline. Therefore, you may have to learn how to
get through your project without any help from the top, even when you
need and expect it.

You could approach an executive for assistance when you cannot
resolve a scheduling conflict, when your team is not capable of completing the task, when you need to expand the budget, or when another
manager refuses to cooperate with you. But don't be surprised if you
run into one or more of these points of view when you ask for help:

- *"It's your project, and you have to solve your own problems."* The
executive may not use these words, but the message will be clear: "I
trusted you with the assignment, and this is just one of the problems
you have to overcome." If this is his or her attitude, you will simply have
to accept it and survive the project without help from the top, no matter
what conflicts you're facing.

- *"If you don't get cooperation from other departments, let me know and
I'll make them help."* While this may seem like the most supportive
stance, be careful. A well-intentioned executive could do more harm
than good by bearing down on a manager who is resisting work with
you—burning any bridge you might be able to create on your own. If
you ask the executive to use power or force to help, you'll run into
problems now and for all future projects. So try to resolve conflicts
without asking for help from a powerful ally, even one with the best of
intentions.

■ *"I'd like to help, but there's really nothing I can do."* This message may be delivered by an executive who simply doesn't want to get involved in conflict. Or, he or she may be experienced enough to know that taking action will only lead to more conflict. By forcing you to come up with a solution, even when it is not easy or obvious, the executive may help you to become a more effective leader.

■ *"Don't make waves. Just do your best to work around the problem."* As passive as this sounds, it may be the best advice of all. Project managers should be good, action-oriented leaders who get results. But at the same time, they must be diplomats, recognizing that their actions have consequences. If you force another manager to provide employees for your team, and if that involves setting your priorities above those of his or her department, the consequences for this and future projects may be more severe than a missed deadline.

DELEGATION PROBLEMS AND SOLUTIONS

As a manager, you are familiar with the process of delegating and monitoring work. As project manager, you still need to delegate. However, the problems you will face may be quite different from those you have in your department, and the solutions should be different as well (see Figure 3-2).

Here are some of the common problems faced by project managers, and ideas for solving them:

■ *Problem: Emphasis is on assignments, not on people.* As a department manager, you are accustomed to facing and overcoming a series of problems. The people working in your department are there on a permanent basis, meaning that their task assignments are usually fixed and well-defined. But as project manager, you face a temporary situation. Problems are unique to the project and nonrecurring in nature. Your team members will not have well-defined areas of responsibility unless you define them.

Solution: Pick the right people, not just the right number. You may find yourself thinking about projects in departmental terms, and this could be a mistake. For example, you know it takes seven people to manage your department's workload, so you conclude that you'll need a specific

Figure 3-2. Delegation problems and solutions.

PROBLEM	SOLUTION
Emphasis is on assignments and not on people.	Pick the right people and not just the right number.
A highly struc- tured working environment is imposed on the team.	Encourage indi- vidual respon- sibility and effort.
The leader is too involved and too assertive.	Lead your team in a different way.
The team is isolated due to lack of delegation.	Coach the team but allow it the freedom to act.
Team members let their egos rule.	Stress team and project goals over indi- vidual success.

number of people for your project, the number becomes the emphasis. An alternative is to pick the people first and then match them to the phases and tasks, not by number, but by areas of responsibility.

■ *Problem: A highly structured work environment is imposed on the team.* You may have learned from experience that a department works well when every task is clearly defined, even in advance of putting someone on the job. The procedures are well-understood, and the scope and limits of each employee's job are defined, often in writing. But when it comes to projects, you will want to encourage people to work more independently, perhaps even with much more freedom than you would ever allow in your department. Imposing an overly structured environment on your team members may stifle their freedom to act and impede the creativity and team spirit you want to encourage.

Solution: Encourage individual responsibility and effort. Team members respond best when they are allowed a degree of independence. Teamwork, ironically, often grows from allowing people to solve problems as individuals. They can work together when the restrictions of a well-defined department are removed. Give your team the freedom to tackle an area of responsibility and to see it through.

■ *Problem: The leader is too involved and too assertive.* You might be what is called a hands-on manager, one who likes to roll up your sleeves and do your share of the work. That approach is appropriate in many departments, and it keeps you in touch with your permanent staff. But for a project, such an approach could impede progress. If you insist that the project be done your way, you are not allowing a team to form. That requires a less assertive approach.

Solution: Lead your team in a different way. Think of your project team differently from how you think of your department. Reduce your role to that of monitor. Watch the budget and the schedule, and ensure that your team comes through; be available to solve problems that your team *wants* you to solve. For some projects, you may need to work on the same level as your team because of deadline pressures, lack of people on your team, or unexpected problems and delays. But step in only if your team needs you, not because you assume that's always the best way to proceed.

■ *Problem: The team is isolated through lack of delegation.* Project management is an excellent opportunity for sharpening your delegation skills. If you do not delegate effectively, your team will sense that it's being left out of the primary work of the project, and everyone will feel isolated. Just as a department manager has to keep staff informed of changes that affect them, you should plan to involve your project team in every phase of the job.

Solution: Coach the team, but allow it the freedom to act. It would be a disaster for a sports coach to take the place of a player because the job wasn't being done correctly. If you see one or more team members failing in their areas of responsibility, don't step in and do the work yourself. Work closely with them, not only to help them complete tasks, but to enable them to recognize the phase and project goals in operation. Help your team to succeed instead of allowing delegation to work in reverse.

■ *Problem: Team members let their egos rule.* You face a difficult challenge when your team stops operating as a unit and becomes a group of individuals in conflict. When team members begin to compete with one another for credit, for work, or for the way to proceed, recognize that the problem is not theirs, it's yours. A team run on ego cannot function well. The intended goal is replaced with personal goals, and your project is in jeopardy of being lost in the shuffle.

Solution: Stress team and project goals over individual success. As team leader, you are responsible for the motives and goals of your team. You may have to remind your team members more than once that they are heading for a common goal and that individual credit or recognition has no place in your project team. You can get the point across by example: Don't present the job as *your* project, or its success or failure in terms of *your* career. It is a team effort, and you will be most likely to succeed when you demonstrate that belief through your own actions.

It has been important to address the personal element of your project before going on to discuss the budget and the schedule. The structure of your team will define these other requirements to a large degree, and your success as a project manager will depend on the people you select and the way in which they work together or are allowed to create on their own team. Chapter 4, shows how the budget fits into the organizational plan of your project.

WORK PROJECT

1. List three ideas for solving the problem of having a project team imposed on you, and explain how this problem can be solved.
2. Explain why the "area of responsibility" approach is different from assigning tasks to team members.
3. Why should you always assume that an outside department's priorities must come first?

4

The Project Budget

If at first you don't succeed, you are running about average.

—M. H. Alderson

"I don't get it," one manager complained to the other. "No matter how carefully I budget, my projects always seem to run over. Even when I add a little extra, it just gets used up."

The other manager responded, "Maybe you should get out of the business world, and go into politics."

If budgeting at any level mystifies and frustrates you, you're in good company. But remember, a budget is only an estimate, and you will impose too high a standard on yourself if you expect actual results to come out exactly as you predict. Also, a budget is only one of your project management tools.

And since you don't have a crystal ball to predict the future, you can only calculate the best possible estimate for a project on the basis of a reasonable schedule, known resources, and management's expectations. These elements, if properly coordinated, will lead to a reasonable budget that you can use to guide your way through the project maze.

BUDGETING RESPONSIBILITY

The budgeting process creates a great deal of pressure, not only for project managers, but for departments, divisions, and subsidiaries. There

49

is an implied test of fiscal success built into the budgeting process: If you meet or come in under the budget, you're assumed to be doing a good job; if you exceed the budget, you're not.

This is unfair if the original budget (it may have been developed under pressure) is unrealistic or imposes a standard that simply can't be met.

Example: A project manager agrees to a budget that is obviously inadequate given the time and resource demands of the project. When actual results run well over the budget, he must explain the problem—even though the budget was imposed from above and arbitrarily set at too low a level.

Remember the purpose of the project budget: to estimate *at a reasonable level* what the project will actually cost the company. You may find it convenient to agree to an inadequate budget at the formation stage, but you will pay for that convenience not only by having to explain variances to top management but by how you will be perceived as a project manager.

You should always develop your own project budget, for several reasons:

1. *You will be responsible for explaining future project expense and cost variances.* That's not possible if you're working with an imposed budget.

2. *As project manager, you are in the best position to know what the project should cost.* The budget you develop is a financially stated goal, and it should serve a purpose on two levels: (1) to give you a means for measuring success during the project and (2) to serve as a way to measure your performance as a project manager.

3. *You will also be able to develop the assumptions that go into the budgeted numbers.* This is essential if any future variance explanations are to make sense. The assumption is compared to actual, and precise differences are isolated. Only when you can compare on this level will the budgeting process work as intended.

Project budgets are developed, monitored, and acted upon differently from departmental or companywide budgets because:

1. *Projects are nonrecurring.* Departmental budgets are prepared each and every year, and often are revised every six months (or even more frequently). Projects, though, are finite activities; the budget time frame is not tied to the fiscal year. Thus, project budget revisions are not likely to occur except as a result of discovering a drastic error in the original budget or in response to a drastic change in the scope of the project.

2. *You have more direct control.* Departmental budgets are often affected by coordination between several departments: The accounting department allocates fixed expenses to one department, often on the basis of estimates of another department; but decisions concerning systems and personnel are restricted to top management. The project, in comparison, involves budgeting on two levels: (1) use of existing resources—personnel and assets—that are already budgeted for at the departmental level and (2) limited use of outside resources that will not be permanent. An additional employee for your department usually translates into a permanent addition to your expense level; an additional employee for a project most likely involves using someone already on hand.

3. *The success of the budget is tied to scheduling and to resource performance.* The success of your project budget depends on how well you schedule each phase and on whether or not the people on your team complete their tasks according to that schedule. If a phase is delayed because you need more time and more human effort than estimated, your budget will reflect an unfavorable variance.

4. *The cost and profit factors in projects may be more obvious than the same factors in a departmental budget.* Unfavorable variances in a project budget may be noticed more than similar, or even more drastic, variances on the departmental level. Your recurring departmental budget is reviewed as part of a larger company budget and forecast; variances may be overlooked, absorbed between departments, or accepted as inevitable—especially if the budget was estimated by one department and then imposed on another. But as project manager, you may be held accountable at a higher level, if only because you're responsible for attaining the cost goals of the project.

It's true that the same standard should apply to every department manager—ideally. Each manager should be responsible for ensuring that the budgeted levels of his or her department are not exceeded. But in practice, few companies exercise the kind of follow-up that would allow such a procedure to be put into action. And few companies allow department managers the level of involvement in budgeting that would make accountability practical.

LABOR EXPENSE: THE PRIMARY FACTOR

In any discussion of a project budget, top management usually begins by asking, "What should this project cost, and is that reasonable?" If the project is optional, the decision to proceed should be based on an estimate of expenses versus future profits. For example, Will the effort reduce operating expenses? Is the project really necessary?

The only way to answer these questions is to identify the true cost of the project. Your estimate must include labor expense—the cost of paying members of your project team. This is usually the most significant part of the project budget, but it's often left out of the budget altogether.

Example: A project manager is asked to estimate the expenses for using an outside consultant, researching historical financial results, and leasing equipment needed for the project. In addition, she is authorized to recruit a team of five people from the company's payroll. However, the payroll cost is not considered in the budget.

The real cost of the project depends largely on the time it will take to complete the tasks. If the project team includes ten members, the labor cost will be higher (meaning the scope of the job will be higher, too). Yet management reasons that it isn't necessary to include labor in the budget because the team members are already on payroll. The cost of paying employees is already on the books and included in each department's budget.

Here are three recommendations concerning project budgeting for labor:

1. *Don't overlook the labor expense of the project.* Even when team members come from within the company, and even though people will

be paid whether the project proceeds or not, you need to isolate the project's total cost to the company on a realistic basis.

2. *Don't add a "fudge factor" to labor—or to any other segment of your budget.* Remember, the purpose of the budget is to estimate the likely expense of the project. Fudge factors are added to protect against the unfavorable variance, should it occur. Adding this factor is contrary to the purpose your budget should serve.

3. *Develop the labor estimate before the project team is selected.* The labor requirements of each phase should dictate the size and scope of the team, not than the other way around. Begin budgeting for labor by estimating the hours required to complete each phase. This should be broken down by individual. Use a worksheet like the one shown in Figure 4-1 to write down the number of hours needed during each phase of the project and break them down according to the special talents you will need in the

Figure 4-1. Preliminary labor estimate.

Project _____

TEAM MEMBER	PHASE							
Total								

phase. This defines the needed resource pool. You may need to consult with team members to ensure that your estimate is realistic.

Example: As manager of a technical support department, your recurring tasks include the development of systems, procedures, and controls for various other departments. Now you have been assigned the project of designing internal procedures for a newly installed computer system that is going into a processing area of the company. You will need to develop a schedule and budget and identify needed team members. You break the project into seven distinct phases and identify team members as follows:

- An employee from the processing area
- An employee from the data processing department
- Three employees from your department, whose responsibilities will be broken down into:
  —Research
  —Documentation
  —Testing

You develop a preliminary estimate of the hours required for each of the seven phases (although after consulting with team members, you may need to alter both the labor estimate and the scheduling time). Your preliminary labor estimate looks like this:

Preliminary Labor Estimate (hours) Project: Automation, processing unit							
				Phase			
Team Member	1	2	3	4	5	6	7
Project manager	23	22	8	25	30	24	40
Processing unit	6	18	25	10	5	0	0
Data processing	20	25	25	20	10	5	5
Research	15	15	20	5	0	0	5
Documentation	0	0	10	10	15	20	35
Testing	0	0	0	5	25	15	10
Total	64	80	88	75	85	64	95

The labor cost is likely to represent the largest portion of the total project budget. It doesn't matter that team members are available and already budgeted for at the department level; the real cost of the project can be revealed only when the project is treated as a separate effort—meaning that the labor expense is budgeted.

ADDITIONAL BUDGETING SEGMENTS

Many projects are characterized exclusively by the labor factor, notably when all tasks are administrative. However, some projects require using resources and facilities in addition to human effort. Therefore, additional budgeting allowances may be needed for:

1. *Fixed overhead allocation.* Some companies may decide, as a matter of accounting policy, to allocate a degree of fixed overhead expenses to a project, especially for long-term projects that will demand considerable floor space. (For example, a project may be set up like a department while the team is operating.)

Fixed overhead allocation is done by formula. For example, departments are allocated portions of utility, maintenance, and other expenses on the basis of the square footage in their areas or the number of employees in the department. It can be argued that this procedure shouldn't apply to projects, especially when allocation has already been made on a departmental basis. However, if a complete cost accounting approach is applied in your company, you will need to include allocated expenses in your project budget.

2. *Variable expenses.* Some projects are accounted for in the same manner as departments. Their expenses are isolated and reported apart from expenses incurred by other departments or projects. A longer-term project may even be assigned a cost center in the company books. You should budget for vairance expenses that will apply, by phase and for the entire project.

You should also assume that fixed expenses either will be treated by allocation or will not be considered as part of your budget.

3. *Special expenses.* The third area to budget is special expense

commitments. This will depend on the nature of your project. For example, you may need to retain an outside consultant, use an independent computer service, or lease equipment for your project.

Some internal departments may contribute to your project in ways other than direct labor. For example, your data processing department may be required to dedicate several days of processing and testing time. This is not labor, but a special service. It should be given a budget value and taken into the total expense equation of your project.

When a series of projects begin to take on similar attributes, they are executed by formula. They then become routines, and project management evolves into a departmental function. But most projects are budgeted individually.

By its nature, a project is a one-time effort and is unlike any previous activity, so you will probably need to create budgets for labor, allocated fixed expenses, and variable expenses by phase. This method is preferable to the alternative: using a formular tied to labor expenses. For example, some project budgets for variable expenses involve computing a percentage of labor costs. The problem with this method is that the variable expense levels for two projects will *not* be identical. Thus, the formula may not work.

Example: A project manager is working on a budget for a job estimated to take six months. His variable expenses are based on historical expense levels. Variable expenses for past projects have averaged 15 percent of labor.

The problem with percentage formulas is that the nature of a new project will be different. Chances are, the actual requirement for variable expenses will depend largely on the nature of the job, not on historical averages. When variances—favorable or unfavorable—do occur, the project manager will not be able to give a meaningful explanation. The only comment he could make would be, "We assumed that variable expenses would be 15 percent of labor; to date, they are averaging 20 percent of labor."

This explanation does not indicate the source of the problem, nor does it lead to a likely solution. If a budget is not built upon any assumption beyond the historical, he cannot tell how to solve the problem—assuming that, for this particular project, there even *is* a problem. What if 20 percent is more appropriate? If so, the error is not in spending levels but in the budget assumption itself.

BUDGETING EACH PHASE

An effective budget should enable you to monitor progress at each phase and to identify precisely when and why actual expenses vary from your estimate. Thus, your budget cannot be constructed on an overall project basis; it needs to be broken down by phase.

All of the budget elements—labor, fixed expenses, and variable expenses—will vary according to the demands of each phase. Some phases will move along relatively quickly and will require minimal team involvement and little or no expense. Others will run to many hours, involve the use of internal and external resources and facilities, and need more detailed monitoring.

To identify problems expressed as budget variances, you must match actual results to the assumptions underlying your budget. So if you assume that one phase will require fifteen hours from an outside consultant, and actual comes in at twenty-two hours, you will be able to identify the exact cause of the variance.

Breaking down your budget by phases also allows you to identify timing differences, time overruns, and miscalculations of the scope of a particular task. This becomes a critical requirement when monitoring your budget. Some expenses may be well under budget, while others are running above it. Identifying the causes of the variances requires matching estimates of phase completion with actual completion.

For example, you may have eight phases in your budget. When you have completed phase 2, should your variable expenses and labor equal 25 percent of the total? Not necessarily. The best way to break down the total project budget is on the basis of percentage-of-completion work. As long as labor represents the lion's share of your expense, the completion phase may be defined by total hours in each phase.

The labor-tied method also dictates percentage-of-completion for other expenses, even when expenses do not always follow the same pattern as labor. However, two points offset this disadvantage: First, it is highly probable that expense trends will follow labor trends (meaning higher expenses will occur in those phases with a higher concentration of labor). Second, if expense variances occur as timing differences due to a labor-connected breakdown, that is an adequate explanation on the variance report.

Example: In the preliminary labor estimate discussed earlier in this chapter, there were seven phases and estimates of labor hours per phase. To identify the budgeted percentage-of-completion for each phase, divide the number of hours in each phase by the total number of hours, and round to the nearest full percentage, as show here:

Phase	Hours	Percentage
1	64	12%
2	80	14%
3	88	16%
4	75	14%
5	85	15%
6	64	12%
7	95	17%
Total	551	100%

Remember, we are assuming that nonlabor expenses are likely to follow the percentage-of-completion trend reflected in labor. In those instances where expenses occur in a different pattern, the variance report should be footnoted; or the variance explanation itself can point to the timing difference between completion phase (based on labor) and non-labor expense timing.

A percentage-of-completion variance report is prepared on the basis of the phases completed to date. A worksheet for this is shown in Figure 4-2.

The estimated percentage-of-completion for each phase is cumulative. Thus, at the end of phase 2, the to-date completion is 26 percent (12 plus 14); and at the end of phase 3, the to-date completion is 42 percent (12 plus 14 plus 16).

Now let's assume that the budget for this project is broken down into these groups:

Labor	$8,200
Variable expenses	1,250
Consulting	2,000
Total budget	$11,450

Figure 4-2. Variance report.

A completed worksheet at the end of the third phase (when 42 percent should be completed) may look like this (note that amounts are rounded to the nearest $25):

VARIANCE REPORT

Date _____5-31_____

Project _Automate processing unit_

Completion ___42___ %

Description	Budget	Actual	Variance Amount	Percentage
Labor	$3,450	$3,135	$ 315	10.0%
Variable expenses	525	615	(90)	(14.6)
Consulting	840	0	840	100.0
Total	$4,815	$3,750	$1,065	28.4%

The Budget column is computed by multiplying the total budget by the indicated percentage complete (42 percent). Actual expenses to date are compared to the project-to-date budget. A favorable variance (when actual is lower than budget) is unbracketed; and an unfavorable variance (when actual is higher than budget) is shown in brackets. Accompanying this summary sheet is a full explanation of the variances in each area. For example, the labor budget explanation may be broken down by team member.

Remember that the purpose of this exercise is to isolate variances by team member. The overall variance is relatively meaningless unless we first understand its components. In the table below, an overall variance of 13 hours seems fairly small. However, the −21 hour variance in Research is very significant.

LABOR VARIANCE, HOURS

| Team Member | Hours, Project-to-Date | | |
	Budgeted	Actual	Variance
Project manager	53	37	16
Processing unit	49	42	7
Data processing	70	61	9
Research	50	71	(21)
Documentation	10	8	2
Testing	0	0	0
Total hours	232	219	13

Explanation: The initial three phases demanded more time than anticipated for organizing and defining automation processes. This was offset by a delay in research activities.

This summary does show how and why the labor variance occurred; that variance may be absorbed in future phases, or it may have to be accepted as a miscalculation in the original estimate. The problem may involve not only past variances, but could also indicate a continuing problem that will affect future phases. You could discover that the final deadline itself cannot be met without making some scheduling changes now.

The hours variance is next translated to dollar amounts, if necessary. The additional detail can be summarized in a table:

LABOR VARIANCE, DOLLARS			
	Dollars, Project to Date		
Team Member	Budgeted	Actual	Variance
Project manager	$1,160	$814	$346
Processing unit	600	504	96
Data processing	840	702	138
Research	700	995	(295)
Documentation	150	120	30
Testing	0	0	0
Total	$3,450	$3,135	$315

If you report your project budget variances as part of a periodic review, it might be a good idea to break down the labor variance in both ways, even if that level of detail has not been requested. With the added information, you will be able to better respond if your budget and actual variances are questioned, or if someone in the review meeting wants to see more detail.

BUDGETING CONTROLS

The identification and reporting of variances may occur in one of two ways: presenting a report on the status of your project and explaining variances to date to top management when they will oversee your management efforts; or using the procedure for yourself to track the budget and take corrective actions—even if you do not need to report on your progress to anyone else.

Either the executive supervising your project determines or requests action when you give your report, or you identify needed actions yourself and take them on your own. If you do present a monthly report, prepare by identifying the needed action and then proposing it as part of the report you present.

Here are some examples of the types of problems revealed in a budget, together with the actions you should take:

■ *Problem: Labor expenses are exceeding budget.* The cause of this problem may be that phases are taking longer than estimated. Several actions should be taken:

Solution 1: Examine the budget for the remainder of the project to determine whether those estimates are also wrong. If they are, you will need to revise the total project expense budget.

Solution 2: Determine whether any of the unfavorable variances can be absorbed in the future. In some instances, a project-to-date variance in labor is the result of advance work on future phases.

Solution 3: Check your own supervisory involvement. You may be able to complete phases more efficiently by working more closely with your team members.

■ *Problem: Variable expenses are exceeding budgeted levels.* This may occur because original assumptions were wrong or because you are not exercising enough control over spending. Consider these actions:

Solution 1: Check original assumptions against experience to date. Are the assumptions still valid? If not, you may need to revise the budget.

Solution 2: Determine whether any of the expenses to date will be absorbed during later phases. If so, the variance may be considered a timing difference.

Solution 3: Initiate needed controls in the same manner that you enforce spending limits in your department. For a long-term project, this may involve preapproval of requisitions or check requests.

■ *Problem: Expenses are lower than the budget, and seem not to be due to timing.* Some project managers budget very conservatively in their departments but build a higher level of safety into project budgets.

Solution: See if you are adding a "fudge factor" in anticipation of possible variances. If so, avoid this in future projects. Your budget is not expected to accurately predict the future; it should be a dependable means for monitoring actual results. Thus, a safety factor added into a budget prevents real control.

The budget, of course, is tied closely to scheduling. For example, if your schedule is unrealistic, you may need to demand more work from team members. Thus, labor expenses will exceed the labor budget.

WORK PROJECT

1. You are preparing a labor budget for your project. You have defined four separate phases, and your team contains five members. Your initial estimate of hours is summarized as follows:

Team Member	Phase 1	2	3	4
1	10	15	15	25
2	8	8	6	12
3	0	15	25	20
4	0	20	20	25
5	10	5	10	15
Total	28	63	76	97

   What is the percentage-of-completion for each phase? Show individual phase and cumulative percentages.

2. Your team members earn varying amounts on a per-hour basis, broken down as:

Team Member	Hourly Payroll
1	$20.00
2	15.00
3	18.00
4	9.00
5	10.00

   Calculate the total amount of labor budget for each phase of the project.

3. You have estimated a total of $2,800 for nonlabor expenses during your project. Based on labor percentage-of-completion, what is the budget for each phase?

5

Establishing a Schedule

To climb steep hills requires slow pace at first.

—William Shakespeare

The project manager called a team meeting for 9 A.M. the next morning. "Don't be late," he said sternly. "We'll be discussing the project schedule."

The team assembled promptly at 9 A.M. as instructed. But the manager was nowhere to be seen. At 9:20, one of the team members called the manager's home and asked for him.

"He'll be a little bit late this morning," the manager's wife explained. "He missed the bus."

Your project ran over budget, you didn't have the right people on the team, and you missed the final deadline. In fact, you took a vacation in Beirut so you wouldn't be there when your boss found out.

If this describes your past experiences as a project manager—or your fear about future projects—then you need to identify methods for planning and controlling your schedule. A schedule is your time budget, just as the proper selection of a team is your resource budget. If you don't plan, coordinate, and control the schedule, your project probably won't be finished on time. In this chapter, you'll learn the proper use of scheduling techniques for anticipating and solving problems, and you'll discover how to get your team working together on a single schedule for each phase of the project.

THE SCHEDULING PROBLEM

If you could work as a team of one, you wouldn't need to coordinate other people's efforts and phase deadlines; instead you could plan, control, and achieve the entire task on your own. In fact, that's how singular functions are executed.

When you are working with a team, however, you need to plan your schedule with an awareness of the networking requirements of that team. For example, your team members may agree to the schedule you devise and proceed with phase 1. But it takes only one delay to throw the entire schedule off, and without your continual supervision, that delay may very well take place.

A small delay within a phase would not be a big problem if it could be isolated. But that delay is likely to affect all of the remaining phases as well as the ability of the rest of the team to succeed. So remember these points concerning delays:

1. *Every delay affects scheduling for the remainder of the project.* Some projects start out with chronic delays. If you don't begin phase 1 on the scheduled date, you will probably encounter problems all the way through. Be sure to schedule realistically; then follow it carefully. Your ability to keep the project on schedule is the real test of your project management skills.

2. *To meet your deadline, the delay will have to be absorbed in a later phase.* It's always desirable to build a little insurance into your schedule by allowing more time than you'll really need to complete the project. However, when a deadline is imposed, you don't always have that luxury. Chances are, you will have a difficult enough time meeting the imposed deadline, and there will be little, if any, opportunity to let a phase deadline slide. If the delays occur in an early phase, your team will have to execute later phases in a shorter amount of time than you planned.

3. *It's desirable always to meet the final project deadline, unless that means that the outcome will be incomplete, inaccurate, or short of the desired result.* To make up for a delay, you may need to work your team at a faster pace, look for shortcuts in the original plan, or put in more hours than you originally planned. Thus, the delay could translate into a budget overrun on your project. Your goal should be to meet the deadline you have promised, unless that means having to cut quality corners. Your project should end with an accurate and high-quality report, implemented procedures, or other results—even if that means you have to ask for an extension.

4. *Staying on schedule and meeting the deadline is the project manager's job.* If you miss your deadline, you may be asked for an explanation. If that occurs, remember that delays are your responsibility, regardless of the cause. Project managers are expected to monitor progress, anticipate problems before they create delays, and take action to prevent missing the final deadline.

Your initial schedule can be expressed on a chart, which is a visual expression of the project's goal. Reducing the project schedule to visual form improves your team's understanding of how the project will progress and gives you the monitoring tool you need. The chart should report both the planned and actual outcomes of each phase, and serves a number of purposes:

1. It is your primary tracking tool, at least in the initial scheduling phase.
2. It provides every team member with schedule guidance and goals.
3. It gives you and your team an ongoing means for spotting and overcoming emerging problems.

The schedule chart also helps you to montior your project methodically—a task that, without some form of management and planning aid, is formidable. The overall scope of a project may be overwhelming, but the chart enables you to isolate immediate problems and to solve them, while keeping the overall schedule. The final deadline is met when you are able to meet a series of smaller phase deadlines—or to absorb scheduling problems in one phase by making them up in another.

THE GANTT CHART

Initial scheduling is effectively planned and tracked by use of the Gantt chart. This device, also called the time-line or milestone chart, was first developed and used by industrial engineer and management authority Henry Gantt.

Gantt worked with the Army Bureau of Ordnance during World War I, and was faced with the need to control daily scheduling of munitions production. He realized that the process could be broken down into precise phases and that many phases could be executed concurrently, in whole or in part. By organizing processes with this in mind, a schedule's efficiency could be maximized. He also realized that this would be most easily communicated with a visual representation of a process and its phases. With this in mind, the Gantt chart was developed.

A Gantt chart can be constructed in a variety of ways, using blacked-in boxes, lines, or symbols. It lets you compare the schedule to actual completion for any project by listing beginning and ending dates of each phase along a time line. Phases are listed from top to bottom, and time is shown from left to right. After each phase is entered on the chart, its progress is tracked.

The chart can be built by hand, put into a computer on a spreadsheet or time management program, or represented on a scheduling board with each phase placed on magnetic strips. However, remember that the chart is not just for your own use. It's most effective when you *and* your team are able to use it to plan and control the project.

In order to demonstrate how the Gantt chart works, we will work through a sample project.

Example: The accounting manager undertakes a project to investigate current procedures in the accounts payable department. She will identify changes needed to improve efficiency and reduce processing expenses, concluding with specific procedures for revision. Her team consists of the accounting manager, the supervisor of the accounts payable department, and a senior-level programming employee from the EDP department.

The manager's first step is to break down the project into phases, as follows:

Phase 1: Document current procedures for each of three employees in the department. *Estimated completion time:* four days.

Phase 2: Prepare procedure flowcharts for the department. *Estimated completion time:* three days.

Phase 3: Summarize paper flow and methods for receiving, processing, and sending out information (including timing, approval, and payment of bills). *Estimated completion time:* five days.

Phase 4: List problem areas and devise initial recommendations for solutions. *Estimated completion time:* six days.

Phase 5: Devise improved procedures for processing. *Estimated completion time:* three days.

Phase 6: Track sample transactions for one week under existing procedures. *Estimated completion time:* five days.

Phase 7: Track sample transactions for two weeks under proposed new procedures. *Estimated completion time:* ten days.

Phase 8: Prepare and deliver a final report to the treasurer, including recommendations for changes in procedures, estimate of savings, and automation if applicable. *Estimated completion time:* two days.

This listing of phases can be expressed on a Gantt chart using the most common method, the bar form. The schedule for this project, including both planned and actual completion for each phase, is shown in Figure 5-1.

Note that the planned phases are listed as clear bars, and those actually completed are blackened. This method shows where delays occurred during execution of the project, and gives the manager and the team a preliminary idea of problems that must be absorbed later on. Phase 1, for example, has taken longer than scheduled, thus delaying phase 2. That delay is carried through all the way to phases 6 and 7, where it is absorbed in time to prepare and deliver the final report.

Note that some phases can be run concurrently. For example, the longest phases (6 and 7) involve testing existing and proposed new procedures. These tests are conducted during the same period, and the initial plan is revised. A shorter time span is used for the tests so that the project can be brought back on schedule before the deadline.

Figure 5-1.   Gantt chart (bar form).

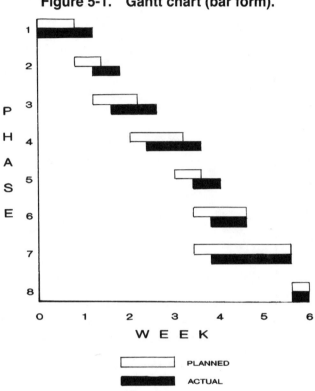

An alternative method of constructing a Gantt chart is to use symbols instead of bars. For example, an unfilled triangle represents the plan, and a filled-in triangle represents actual. The start date is shown by a triangle with the base at the bottom, and the completion date of each phase is represented by an inverted triangle. A Gantt chart of this type, using the same project example, is shown in Figure 5-2.

Triangles can be placed on a single line for each phase or, as in our example, on different lines, allowing a separation between planned and actual status. This method provides a bit more information than the bar form, but you may find it more difficult to quickly grasp the degree of variance for the overall project that is created when one phase is delayed by a few days.

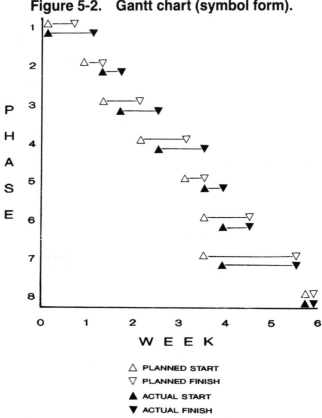

Figure 5-2.   Gantt chart (symbol form).

A third version is similar to the first, in that it uses a series of bars for each phase. However, rather than simply representing phases by overall duration, each phase is broken down into subphases. These are identified in Figure 5-3 with alphabetical symbols.

For example, in phase 1, the a–b–c division may represent documentation of procedures for each of three employees working in the department under study. The subphasing technique is especially useful for complex projects where phase control requires a detailed breakdown and, perhaps, coordination of two or more team members. If the duration and scope of work within each phase is complex enough, a

Figure 5-3. Gantt chart (fill-in form).

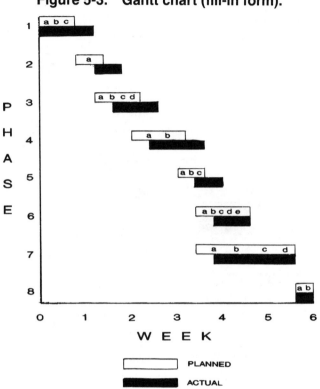

subdivision will help you to manage and supervise the work of your team.

Another benefit of the fill-in method is that an ongoing phase can be reported and tracked by degress of completion. For example, a phase is about half-completed, but the deadline is coming up in two days. By darkening half of the "actual" segment for that phase, the problem is highlighted and identified.

SCHEDULING CONTROL

The more planning you put into developing your initial schedule, the better the chances for meeting deadlines later on. In addition, you should plan to go over your proposed schedule with each team member. Carefully check to ensure that your team is confident that the schedule can be met—so that timing for the final deadline will not become a problem later.

Follow the steps shown here and in Figure 5-4 to create your project schedule:

1. *Identify phases.* Break your project down into logical phases. These will come to represent specific, distinct areas of effort and team responsibility. Thus, each phase should be characterized by specializa-

Figure 5-4.   Creating the schedule.

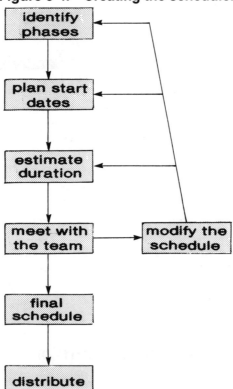

tion, its dependence on prior phase completion, and its necessity for phases yet to come.

2. *Plan start dates.* Decide which phases must be executed consecutively, and which can be executed concurrently. In some cases, a phase cannot be started until a previous one has been completed. In others, you can begin work while previous phases are still in operation.

3. *Estimate the duration of each phase.* Next, decide how many days or weeks will be needed to complete each phase. (Basing your schedule on a preliminary estimate of hours required to complete each phase is an acceptable method that can be used at this step; however, be prepared to impose completion deadlines before finalizing the schedule.) Remember to overlap phases when they can operate concurrently.

4. *Meet with the team.* Involve your team members in the schedule plannng step; otherwise, they cannot be expected to work together cooperatively. Just as you should be allowed to establish your own final project deadline when an assignment is given to you, your team should be allowed to participate in defining the time requirements for each phase.

5. *Modify the schedule as needed.* Listen to what your team tells you. If members responsibile for a phase state that the deadline is unrealistic, seek solutions. Where necessary, modify your schedule according to your team's response.

6. *Prepare the schedule.* Construct the Gantt chart you will use to track the schedule. As the project moves along, the actual should be entered on the chart. Keep up the monitoring and summary of the project so that you will be able to take action if and when delays occur.

7. *Distribute the schedule.* Once you have finalized your schedule and made up the Gantt chart, send a copy to each team member. As the project moves ahead, pass out revised and updated copies—probably on a weekly basis. If you are reporting to an executive regarding the project, you can use the Gantt chart as a useful visual summary for your report.

THE SCHEDULING SOLUTION

Even the most efficient, experienced, and capable project manager will eventually face a difficult schedule delay. The delay itself is not a failure;

that's simply part of the team dynamic. The real test is in how well the delay problem is solved when it occurs.

Sometimes you can spot a future problem and take action before a delay occurs.

Example: A team member advises you halfway through a project that departmental priorities will prevent her from executing an upcoming phase according to schedule. At that point, you shift the assignment, complete it in advance of the conflict dates, or simply accept the delay (which will affect the work of the rest of your team). You also negotiate a compromise, either with the team member or with her supervisor.

Once a delay has occurred, take one of the following actions to correct the problem:

1. *Execute phases concurrently when possible, even if your original plan called for consecutive scheduling.* Some phases must be organized and executed consecutively. A later phase cannot be started until the results of the earlier phase are available. In these instances, delays are most troublesome, since your team simply cannot proceed. However, in many other cases, you can begin a subsequent phase even without completion of a prior one.

Example: You are managing a project that will result in automation of a processing department's routines. You run into a delay during an early phase. This phase was intended to define the number of transactions processed during the average month (for the purpose of identifying needed computer file space and input fields). The next phase is to begin writing the input and storage program itself. When the delay occurs, you decide to proceed with the next phase on schedule. Even though the specifics of the program are subject to change, you conclude that most of the program design work can proceed.

2. *Double up your team's effort to absorb the previous delay.* A phase may be the responsibility of one team member, but delays may make it impossible to complete it on schedule. In this instance, you might be able to overcome the problem by assigning other team members to help.

Example: One member of your team is responsible for compiling historical information in order to establish the cost of manual processing (and also to estimate savings that will be achieved with automation). This information is essential to your report. However, due to a previous delay, you want to complete this phase in less than the scheduled time. So you assign a second team member to help gather and summarize historical information.

3. *Begin preliminary steps on future phases to save time later.* You may be frustrated because delays are keeping most of your team idle. You cannot accelerate the phase underway, and you can't begin the next phase until this one is completed. However, you might be able to save time by completing coming phases partially.

Example: Your project will end with a detailed report to management; however, you may not be able to complete the report on time because of a two-day delay near the end of the project schedule (you have allowed your team five working days to complete the report). But you may still be able to meet the deadline by having your team prepare the graphs summarizing the historical information, which will go into the report. These can be prepared now, even though the ongoing phase hasn't been completed.

4. *Seek methods to speed up later phases, without losing quality.* Some late phases in a project may be executed in a shorter time span than originally scheduled. This is the most likely way to make up delays created during earlier phases.

Example: You've planned to conclude your project for a system conversion with a three-week test in which both the old processing system and the new one will be operated together. The purpose is to find and correct any bugs. However, you decide to cut the test to two weeks because earlier phase delays have put your team behind schedule. You are certain that you will be able to find and correct any problems during the first week, thus ensuring that the new system works as planned.

The Gantt chart is a simple method for tracking your project. However, it may be of limited use when you must deal with a very large project team (meaning there will be a lot of interaction and networking on a cooperative level) and when the project itself is especially complex. If work will demand a period of several months rather than a few weeks, the Gantt chart may not satisfy the monitoring requirements for the project.

GANTT LIMITATIONS

If your project is complex, you may run into the following problems if the Gantt chart is your only planning tool:

1. *It does not identify potential weak links between phases.* Whenever work is transferred from one person or department to another, your project is subject to potential delay. These weak links are the most common causes of delays.

Example: One team member completes his portion of the work for one phase, but another fails to take up and complete his part by the deadline because the memo or worksheet is buried in an interoffice envelope somewhere on his desk. He did not communicate within the network to find out why the apparent delay had occurred.

2. *It does not reveal the problems your team will encounter due to unexpected delays.* The Gantt chart shows only the planned and actual start and completion dates for each phase. It gives you a quick visual overview of the project's status, but you might need more. The chart does not show how a delay during one phase will impact on the completion of another. Thus, one of the most critical actions you can take—spotting problems and countering them in time—is not always possible by use of the Gantt chart alone.

3. *It does not coordinate the resources or networking requirements needed at critical points in the schedule.* Many projects can proceed only when forms, documents, reports, outside help, and other requirements are either developed by your team or supplied by someone else. Thus, a complete schedule should identify these critical points and enable you to plan ahead for the related demands. The Gantt chart does not provide this much detail.

4. *It does not show the degree of completion for each phase.* You can use the fill-in method and carefully track degrees of phase completion, but generally, the Gantt chart is not designed for detailed tracking; it is intended to be used only as an overview of the entire project. Once you discover an error, you will have to investigate, identify the cause, and correct the problem. By then, the problem has already occurred. Fortunately, there are alternative scheduling techniques that allow you to spot

emerging delays and avoid them—through knowing where the weak links are or being able to anticipate problems.

Use the Gantt chart to define overall scheduling priorities, discuss modifications with your team, track timing goals, and report on the project's success while it's underway. But for more detailed monitoring, you will need more advanced scheduling techniques. These are the subject of Chapter 6.

WORK PROJECT

1. Explain three points concerning delays in project phases, and how they affect the final deadline and your management task.
2. You have been appointed as manager of a newly formed department. One of your first projects is to develop a one-year budget. You have defined the following phases:

Phase

1	Identify assumptions for each expense category.
2	Develop initial budgets for each expense.
3	Cross-reference the budget summary to assumption worksheets.
4	Submit your initial budget for review.
5	Enter revisions.
6	Revise assumption worksheets.
7	Prepare the final departmental budget.
8	Submit the final budget report.

Which of these phases can be executed concurrently, and which must be done consecutively?
3. Explain three possible ways to eliminate delays you might encounter during your project.

6

The Rules of Flowcharting

If you do not think about the future, you cannot have one.

—John Galsworthy

"I'm tracking my project with a method used by the government in a submarine development program," one manager told another. "And now I can really identify with the navy."

"Why, because it helps you keep your project on schedule?" the other manager asked.

"No, because I'm having problems keeping my head above water."

If you have a lot of time, you can develop and use a complicated schedule system to control your project. On the other hand, if time isn't a problem, then neither is the schedule. The secret is to find an effective method that can be put into action quickly but that also gives you the control information you will need every day.

The advantage of the Gantt chart is that it can be put together quickly. If properly tracked, it can also be used to manage time and look for problems—even during a specific phase.

The disadvantage of the Gantt chart is that it does not identify the "weak links": points where information is passed from one person to another within your team; where outside resources are depended on; and where an action cannot be taken until someone else does his or her part. A Gantt chart only shows you when a project phase starts and ends and how it's progressing. You may find that the network of your project team requires a more elaborate tracking system.

LISTING OUT THE PHASES

Chapter 5 presented an eight-phase project for improving procedures in a processing department. In that example, a specific number of phases were broken out and listed in order of precedence. This is the first step in devising the network; however, a problem may arise when you attempt to distinguish between an "event" and an "activity."

An *activity* is the step (or steps) involved at each phase, and an *event* is an end result (e.g., completion of a report) or some other necessary step (e.g., receipt of information from another team member). As a general rule, an activity occurs during a phase, and an event is the end result—or, within the project, the step required in order to proceed to the next phase.

These distinctions are important because they point out a common flaw in flowcharting. The diagram you draw will consist of a series of boxes (or circles) joined by lines. The tendency is to use the boxes to describe activities, meaning the lines are nothing more than connectors between boxes. Where does the time requirement go? You will be confused if the activities reside in the boxes but time estimates are tracked on the lines. It's more accurate to use one of the three other methods:

1. Placing events (end of phases) within the boxes and using the lines in between to describe activities and the time those activities require
2. Isolating activities in the boxes with events placed *below* in a separate box, and using the lines in between to describe the time requirements preceding the events
3. Placing activities in the boxes with events listed *below*, and tracking time on a separate line

The first method is often appropriate for large-scale and exceptionally complex projects (it lends itself well to automated project management). The second method allows you to track activity and time—the critical elements of schedule control—and to isolate events that fall out of those elements. The third method may prove to be the most practical for a manually controlled project of limited duration and relatively small team size.

For any scheduling system more involved than the Gantt chart, begin by organizing phases in sequence, and by task or subtask within each phase. The purpose is to identify the precise order of activities and events. Remember, an activity occurs on the way to achieving completion of each phase. An event is the end of the phase.

For exceptionally complicated phases, scheduling may involve identifying and isolating two or more events that come up at the same time.

Example: You test a new procedure for two weeks. During the test, you compare results to the previous system four times and make any needed adjustments. In this case, the phase is broken down and identified by four separate events within the phase—one for each comparison—and by a final event; completion of the test.

Organizing a project in this way is called Work Breakdown Structuring (WBS), and it can be done using one of two formats.

The Outline Format

First is the outline, or tabular format.

Under the outline format, each phase is a major heading, and details are broken out by subheads. This format helps you in several ways:

1. *You can identify responsibilities by team members.* On the outline itself, each task or series of tasks is first broken out by description. Once you are satisfied with this, the project team member who will have primary responsibility for that task can be assigned a particular phase. If others are involved, they should be identified as well. Thus, starting with the simple outline, the details of responsibility are expanded into a series of defined steps.

2. *You can control time on a detailed level.* The time estimate for each phase should be specified, and subroutines broken out in terms of hours or days estimated for completion. With the outline done, you next map out time requirements and constraints. These may be dictated by team limitations, such as the number of hours each person is able to give to your project within a limited time frame. The time element is a further elaboration of the sequence outline.

3. *You can look for possible weak links in the procedure—points where your involvement might be needed to keep work moving and on schedule.* Identifying weak links—where responsibility passes from one person to another or where you must wait for someone outside your team to supply information—is the key to schedule control. The outline can be used to highlight these points. With this information in hand, you are best-prepared to control your schedule.

Achieving this control is the ultimate benefit of organizing and mapping out your schedule. However, knowing where the weak links occur is only the first step. You need to take two additional steps: (1) bringing the weak link to the attention of two team members—the one who conveys the information and the one who receives it—and (2) following up and supervising the weak link itself to ensure successful and timely action.

Using the procedure revision project introduced in Chapter 5, the outline form looks like this:

Project: Procedure Revisions

1.0 Document current procedures.
    1.1 Interview employees.
    1.2 Review documentation.
    1.3 Update documentation.

2.0 Prepare procedure flow charts.
    2.1 Identify work flow.
    2.2 Coordinate between employees.
    2.4 Review flowcharts.
    2.5 Adjust.

3.0 Summarize paperflow
    3.1 Prepare final workflow.   *(continues)*

3.2 Identify sources.
3.3 Identify destinations.
3.4 List department reports.

4.0 List problem areas and solutions.
4.1 List inefficient areas.
4.2 Identify weak links.
4.3 List possible solutions.
4.4 Summarize solution ideas.

5.0 Devise improved procedures.
5.1 Prepare flowcharts.
5.2 Develop narratives.

6.0 Track sample transactions for one week under existing procedures.
6.1 Identify test area.
6.2 Track daily totals.
6.3 Summarize.
6.4 Prepare summary report.

7.0 Track sample transactions for two weeks under proposed procedures.
7.1 Isolate daily test area.
7.2 Process information.
7.3 Summarize.
7.4 Compare to existing totals.
7.5 Prepare comparison report.
7.6 Adjust new system as needed.

8.0 Prepare and deliver final report
8.1 Explain problem/solution.
8.2 Summarize test data

The Tabular Format

The second method for WBS is the organizational format. The same information is arranged from top to bottom, with each phase broken down much like an organization chart, as shown here:

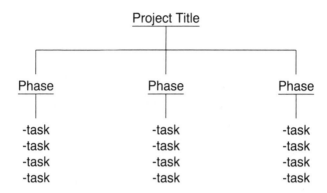

Either method can be employed. You may base your selection on personal preference, the complexity of the project, assignments, or team size. The purpose is to develop project information so that the scheduling controls you need can be mapped out and followed. Once the WBS job is complete, you can prepare a diagram and list activity time requirements.

CPM AND PERT METHODS

Between 1956 and 1958, two scheduling control systems were developed: Critical Path Method (CPM) and Program Evaluation and Review Technique (PERT). Both of these systems were originally designed to track time for projects involving concurrent activity and to monitor and control time expenditures. Since then, CPM and PERT have been expanded and used in many applications on projects, including budgeting, resource management, process definition, and quality control. When the two systems are combined, as they are in many applications, the process is referred to as a PERT/CPM network.

CPM (see Figure 6-1) is a network diagram showing the critical path as well as noncritical junctures and activities. The time estimate for each activity is indentified by a range of start and finish periods (usually in terms of hours or days). This helps you visualize the flow of effort and identify how different segments of one project team must work together to achieve completion of each phase.

Figure 6-1. CPM diagram.

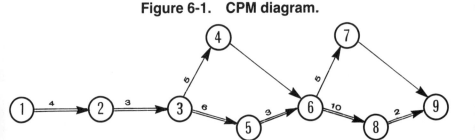

When used for schedule time control alone, CPM tracks several factors: minimum and maximum time required, phase and project-to-date time expended, and identification of earliest start and finish times. Procedures have been developed for calculating these times, and for isolating "floats"—opportunities to make up time variances in the schedule. PERT identifies the time requirements for phases, as well as needed labor resources. It allows for rescheduling of phases with minimal delays, and also improves work flow between team members and outside resources.

PERT involves estimates of minimum, most likely, and maximum time requirements. Calculations of schedule requirements are done by way of a weighted average. Both CPM and PERT may be appropriate for very large scale projects, especially those controlled through a sophisticated computer program for project management. However, for smaller-scale projects operated on the departmental level, PERT/CPM does not provide you with the most useful level of information. PERT/CPM may be too complex for the projects you will encounter.

AUTOMATED PROJECT MANAGEMENT SYSTEMS

Project management, like many other business activities, may be efficiently managed through an automated system—assuming that automation does, in fact, save time and increase your effectiveness.

Automation is a suitable alternative to manual control when a large body of information needs to be managed more efficiently. But, remember, to achieve the desired level of useful results, the information must be input; it must then be verified; as changes occur, it must be modified; and finally, it must be arranged in such a way that you can use it to control the project.

In too many instances, a project's nature as a one-time effort does not lend itself well to many programs advertised as project manager systems. Remember, a computer is designed to manage *consistently* processed information; it does not work as well for exceptions.

Before automating the project management task, consider the problems you may face in these areas:

1. *Cost and time—input time versus the value of results.* If it takes too long to input information, verify and modify it, and get results out of the automated system, ask yourself whether the cost of the system is justified. Would it be faster to coordinate the project by hand? If so, you're better off avoiding automation.

2. *Learning curve.* How much time will it take for you and your team to learn the system? With the great emphasis placed on hardware and software, the need for training and support is too often overlooked. It may be that the energy and investment in training will not justify what could be a marginal benefit from automated project management.

3. *Investment.* You will need to convince management that its investment in hardware, software, and training will be justified by benefits. Considering that projects—unlike departmental tasks—involve exceptions to the usual processing methods, this may be hard to do.

4. *Software.* Remember, the software package you buy for project management should provide the reports, organizational output, and information formats *you* want. If you do not find software that fits your special requirements, you may be tempted to alter your project management system to suit the existing or affordable software. This is a mistake! Why give up a proven system of control just to automate?

The answer to whether or not the right software exists will vary with each case. Even with a system that is satisfactory for this month's project, you may achieve greater efficiency with the system in a different project in the future. The system you apply in managing a project should be modified according to its complexity, scheduling and budget demands, team size, and other attributes. Thus, no one software package will be suited exactly to every project you execute.

Extremely sophisticated systems, designed along the lines of PERT/CPM, are more suited to much larger projects than those you are likely to encounter. They will probably also be far beyond your budget. On the other hand the affordable programs come with limitations and tend to be less flexible.

For example, software programs advertised for project management and offering a wide range of applications cost between $300 and $900. Some imitate the PERT/CPM networking methods, using a rather simplified format, and are of questionable practical value for short-term projects. Other programs in this range—perhaps titled "Project Management"—are, in fact really programs for organizational activity: time management, address files, personal scheduling, word processing, basic reporting and graphics, or combinations of these facilities. While these routines are connected to project management, they are *not* project management programs. You may use them for parts of the overall management function, but not as a replacement for the budgeting and schedule controls you need to apply within projects.

Automation is not a substitute for direct and practical management of your team's schedule, nor does it eliminate the actions you will need to take in correcting time and budget variances. A common error is to automate a function that has presented problems in the past, in the mistaken belief that "the computer will solve the problem."

If you do decide to automate, follow these guidelines:

1. *First solve the problems of management over projects.* Most of the difficulties you will encounter as a project manager have to do with issues you cannot automate: human relations, estimates of time and money, and overcoming obstacles to achieving a desired end result. You cannot improve in these areas exclusively through automation; rather, you must depend largely on experience, intuition, and knowledge, all modified by the facts in each case.

2. *Identify recurring processes that can be better handled through automation.* Within the project management task, certain recurring routines can be automated—not necessarily on an inflexible project management

system as someone else views it but through use of the software designed for organization and storage of large bodies of data.

3. *Automate for efficiency of processing not as a replacement for your direct involvement as project manager.* The most common pitfall is to automate in the belief that existing, nontransactional problems will be solved by the computer. Don't overlook the continuing demand for ongoing direct involvement with your team.

4. *Don't confuse the objectives of the project with objectives of automation.* Another common problem is to forget the real objectives of the project and to become deeply involved in the automated aspect of it. The objective of automation should be to organize information and to make it available in a useful format not to restrict what you can do with information according to program limitations.

5. *Don't change your procedures to suit a program's limitations.* If you can't find suitable software, automation won't make your job any easier; it may only complicate and confine it. The solution, though, is not to abandon sensible procedures because the software can't support them. Instead stick with the best procedure given the nature of the project, and use automation when and where it does help.

6. *Develop a practical, effective system for managing your projects manually.* First, overcome the problems involved with project management; then look for ways to increase your efficiency, either through partial automation or improvement in your monitoring routines.

The most effective method for controlling a project with a limited time constraint and a relatively small team that is isolated to one or two departments probably will not involve a sophisticated computer program. It's more likely that you will gain the most from a flowchart that supplies you with the control mechanisms you need; and the graphic part of project management on a practical level is the least likely output you will get from project management software. Most supply Work Breakdown Structure and Gantt charts. However, these are no more than computerized versions of information you must first develop by hand and then input to the system. You will probably need to progress far beyond these tools on a day-to-day basis.

SETTING YOUR FLOWCHARTING RULES

The essential tool for the project manager is the flowchart. However, the project flowchart you design needs to list much more than activities and sequence. You also need to identify the critical elements of responsibility by team member, time control, events (reports, forms, information supplied by the outside), and coordination of concurrent processes.

For all of this, you need to move away from the restrictions of vertical flowcharting. You also need to set rules for yourself, as follows:

1. *Always use the precedence method.* In order to establish the appropriate sequence of activities and events, the entire project should be arranged in the most logical format. You can identify this by working from an outline (WBS). Does each event fit according to what precedes it and what comes after?

2. *Make sure the path of activities and events makes sense.* The task of building a flowchart is simplified by recognizing that the lines connecting boxes or circles are much more than mere connectors. The path of activities and events works when arranged logically. Every action is generated by a preceding action or event, and leads to a subsequent action or event. No one action can begin without a preceding one, and no action should lead to a dead end.

3. *Remember, an activity cannot occur until a preceding activity or event has been completed.* This rule assumes a direct connection between the current activity and the preceding activity or event. You may also have concurrent activities in different segments of your team. However, when scheduling your project, operate under the precedence constraint on each activity path.

4. *Carefully plot, explain, and control concurrent events.* Team members not accustomed to working from network diagram flowcharts will be confused when a number of concurrent events are taking place. Thus, plan these very carefully, remembering the precedence method and ensuring the logic of the path. You will also need to lead your team through what will look like a maze of activities and events, so be prepared to supervise each phase to ensure that the flowchart is being followed correctly.

5. *Exercise control over weak lines, as this is the key to successful project management.* More than anything else, the flowchart helps you identify the weak links in the process. The greatest threat of delay or error occurs when responsibility for work passes from one person to another. By knowing where the weak links occur, you will remove the scheduling delays that most often characterize projects. As a result of extra care over weak links, you provide the most effective method of project control.

6. *Flowchart decision steps with great care to avoid confusion.* A simple flowchart is not confusing; one step follows another. However, you will encounter decision point where the flowchart breaks into two segments: one for a yes and one for a no decision. Each decision point should be accompanied by a narrative explanation for the team member affected by it. In addition, you should cover that phase with each team member directly to ensure that he or she understands and correctly follows the procedure.

WORK PROJECT

1. Describe three benefits of organizing your schedule using Work Breakdown Structuring (WBS) in outline form.
2. List and explain three guidelines for automating project management.
3. List and explain three rules for flowcharting.

7

The Project Flowchart

It is a capital mistake to theorize before one has data.

—Arthur Conan Doyle

"I gave up on flowcharting after trying it for a while," one manager explained to another. "It was just too complicated."

"What do you mean?" the other one asked. "I find that flowcharting makes it easier to stay on schedule."

"We finished on time. But instead of coming out with the result I expected, we built a radio."

A visual summary of your project helps control the schedule and assign resources. Thus, your goal is to come up with a simple but effective flowcharting method. If it ends up being too complicated, you'll never get around to working on the project.

The Gantt chart will help you to identify the order of activities and events. But unfortunately, that's not all there is to scheduling. The real challenge is in keeping several activities on track at the same time.

Many projects involve complicated interaction among members of your team when a number of activities are going on at the same time. In these cases, a more elaborate and detailed flowcharting method is called for. To be practical, this method should be designed on the precedence method. Your purpose is to devise a system that helps you control and monitor the activities of several people. Since some of those activities will be executed at the same time, you need to act as a coordinator, supervising the activities of several team members or groups. Chances are, if any one of those activities is delayed, the entire project will fall behind schedule.

Imagine how difficult a task you face when your team consists of ten or fifteen people, and five or six different phases are underway at the same time. You have a choice: Either run from one group to another and make sure they all meet their deadlines, or devise a method for keeping track of everything at once—no matter how many activities are taking place.

That goal demands that you also keep track of who is supposed to take responsibility for each activity. One problem with the Gantt chart is that it does not identify the individual team member who will be responsible for an activity or event; the emphasis is on sequence and time requirements. An alternative, the network diagram, gives you more information and combines scheduling and assignments on one form while specifying the precedence of activities and events.

ACTIVITY AND EVENT SEQUENCES

Most people think of flowcharts as moving vertically from a start point at the top to an end point at the bottom. This is the flowcharting method used in describing procedures or in writing programs for new routines. It works well when one person executes a series of steps or when a series of commands follow one another. However, most projects involve several people, often working together on the same phase, or working on different phases but at the same time.

Your purpose is to develop a useful working document for project control. It should incorporate the precedence method, which allows you to coordinate the concurrent efforts of your team as well as the overall schedule. Individual team members are likely to be concerned with the immediate task and phase, whereas you need to constantly keep an eye on the final deadline.

A good starting point is to identify the attributes of events that will occur in your project. In defining activities and events, we make several assumptions:

1. *Events have predetermined sequences.* An event must be completed before a subsequent activity can be undertaken (the precedence method). A future activity should be assumed to depend on completion of a previous event. This situation is called a *singular* event, and it is the simplest form of work completion. If you are solely responsible for a phase, you can break it down into a series of activities and events, one after another.

2. *Events may depend on multiple activities.* Some events do not occur even when a primary activity has been completed—for example, if another team member must also complete a related activity. This is one point where scheduling delays are likely to occur. If you are working toward a phase deadline but are depending on someone else to complete an activity on time, you will be able to meet that deadline only if the other person comes through. This situation is called a *joint* effort: Two or more team members work on related activities, which must be completed before an event can occur.

3. *Activities and events may take place apart from each other.* Some events can occur only after someone else has completed a separate activity. This is another point where delays may occur: A team member responsible for an event can act only after someone else has completed an activity. This is called a *dependent* effort.

The three types of sequencing are summarized in Figure 7-1. Notice that the singular effort occurs on only one line, indicating that one person is responsible for the activities and the events. However, joint and dependent efforts involve two or more people.

These are important distinctions that help you to keep your projects on schedule. The weak links—points where scheduling is most likely to fail—occur where two or more people are involved. Weak links include joint and dependent activities on many levels: where information developed by one person is given to another, where processing is concurrent with a deadline in mind, and where there is a need for information or reports from someone outside of your team (e.g., another department).

THE VERTICAL FLOWCHART

Most people, when asked to prepare a flowchart, will put it into a top-to-bottom format, an acceptable way to describe a project, especially one with few steps and involving a limited number of people.

Figure 7-1. Activities and events.

SINGULAR EFFORT

A)
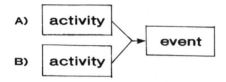

JOINT EFFORT

A)
B)
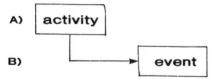

DEPENDENT EFFORT

A) activity

B) event

Using the same example described in Chapter 6 (revising procedures and testing them), the vertical flowchart can be quickly prepared from an outline of the phases, as follows:

Phase	Description
1	Document procedures.
2	Prepare flowcharts.
3	Summarize paper flow.
4	Describe problems and solutions.
5	Design improved procedures.
6	Track the old system for one week.
7	Track the new system for two weeks.
8	Prepare the final report.

Recalling that steps 3 to 4 and steps 6 to 7 are executed during the same period, a vertical flowchart like the one in Figure 7-2 can be prepared.

While this format presents the steps directly and in proper sequence, it also has flaws:

Figure 7-2.   Vertical flowchart.

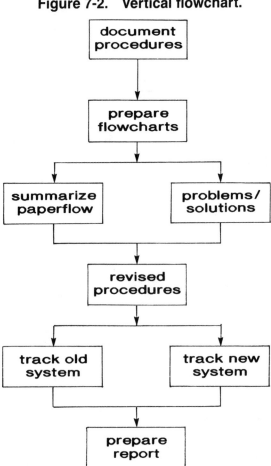

1. It does not show the time requirements for each phase. All the vertical flowchart shows is the sequence of activities.
2. Like the Gantt chart, this method does not give you a breakdown by team member, so there is no division of responsibility.
3. It does not show concurrent activity. Thus, it is not as useful as a Gantt chart, which does illustrate time-concurrent activities.

For effective scheduling control, the vertical flowchart has little value as a control tool. It's really just an outline, expressed in boxes joined by arrows rather than just listed out. However, it is useful as a preliminary step in developing a more practical flowcharting method: the horizontal network diagram.

You may need to prepare a vertical flowchart from your outline just to ensure that the steps are listed in a logical sequence. But for a very complicated project involving many steps, the order of execution may not be obvious from a preliminary list. Any problems in sequencing will probably be discovered as you break down the project into a vertical flowchart.

Example: In developing a schedule for a project to revise procedures, your outline begins with the step, "Describe problems and solutions." However, when you begin to build your flowchart, you realize that other steps must occur first. You will not be able to define the problems completely until you have documented procedures and summarized the paper flow. Thus, you revise the sequence of phases so that those preliminary steps can be completed first.

ADVANTAGES OF HORIZONTAL DIAGRAMS

Using the activity steps from a vertical flowchart, you can add more information. But activity sequence is only the skeleton of your scheduling control. To round it out, you must also identify and track:

- Deadlines for each phase
- Individual team members who will execute each phase
- Weak links—where effort involves two or more people

These goals can be met by constructing a horizontal flowchart, even for the most complex project.

The adventages of horizontal flowcharting are:

1. *It shows interaction between team members.* Project activities and events do not occur in isolation—if they did, each team member could execute his or her phase without the involvement of anyone else. The points of interaction should be your greatest concern, because you need to coordinate the efforts of the team, and not just of individuals. The precedence of activities may include two or more people. Thus you need to make sure that the schedule is followed through each phase, and that requires supervision, notably over weak links.

2. *It establishes an exact sequence.* Attempts to flowchart without application of the precedence method lead to problems. Some projects do not stay on schedule because an exact sequence of events has not been planned out. Thus, you come to a point where you expect an activity to occur, only to discover that a different activity must occur first. And if the team member responsible for that activity is not free at that moment, the entire project comes to a standstill.

3. *It draws attention to the weak links.* Knowing where the weak links are is an important advantage; a horizontal flowchart gives you an immediate overview of these points and shows you where your involvement is most needed.

4. *It breaks down areas of responsibility.* A horizontal flowchart shows all of the activities for each team member. These activity areas are described as *areas of responsibility* rather than in terms of individuals. This is necessary because one person will not always be solely responsible for activities or events. You may break your team into individuals, team units, or small committees for a singular activity. Or, in some cases, a team "member" may actually be an entire department. The horizontal flowchart shows which activities will be executed for each area of responsibility—what each person or group will do during the project.

5. *It shows concurrent activity flow.* Project managers are often overwhelmed by the complexity of team performance. For a complicated project, you may have to oversee a large number of different activities at the same time. If you don't supervise each of these, you may suffer delays. The horizontal flowchart clearly breaks down concurrent activities, enabling you to keep the entire project on course.

6. *It ties actions to time controls.* The horizontal flowchart includes a time line. This combines the best features of the Gantt and vertical flowcharts. When each activity and event is broken down by completion time (hours or days), you will be able to manage the schedule directly.

7. *It lists reports, forms, and other documents.* Many projects require interim and final reports; development of worksheets, forms, and other documents; and documents from other departments. The horizontal flowchart incorporates this requirement.

8. *It aids in communicating with your team.* Schedule control does not take place in the project manager's office only. It depends on a team effort. A horizontal flowchart allows you to better demonstrate to your team where problems might occur, how you plan to solve them, and how different activities will occur at the same time. And team members will be better able to communicate their ideas and concerns to you.

9. *It allows you to detect and correct variances.* As your project moves ahead, you may experience scheduling variances for any number of reasons. That isn't a problem. The real problems come up when you don't have the information you need to find the variance when it occurs or when you don't take action to get the project back on schedule. A horizontal flowchart enables you to spot variances and to find ways to absorb the time overrun. That might involve shifting duties among team members, looking for ways to cut time requirements from a subsequent phase in the schedule, or doubling up the team effort. These solutions are best managed by reviewing the horizontal flowchart and looking for opportunities to solve time variance problems.

10. *It identifies alternatives.* The initial outline and schedule you develop in the form of a Gantt chart or vertical flowchart may seem to be the best way to proceed. But when problems do arise, either in scheduling or in team workload, you need the flexibility to change the original plan. The horizontal flowchart acts as a tool for achieving that flexibility.

BUILDING THE NETWORK DIAGRAM

The horizontal flowchart, or network diagram (see Figure 7-3), is a left-to-right breakdown of each activity. Events are listed beneath the flow section. Arrows connect activity boxes, but only as a means for showing

Figure 7-3. Network diagram format.

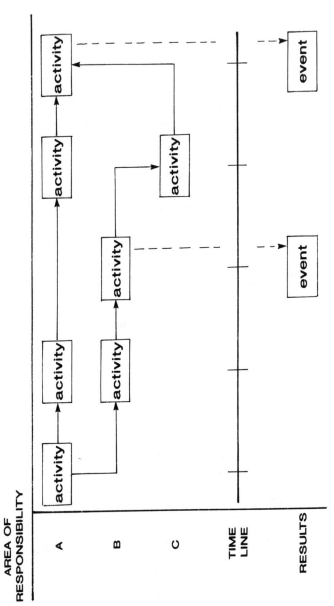

how one action follows another and which actions take place in each area of responsibility.

Each box is an activity, with events listed below in a separate section. This makes sense. For example, in preparing a report, the process of preparation is the activity and the report is the result. The result does not require a step; thus, it can be listed directly beneath the activity box.

This format provides you with all of the scheduling and control information you need. For example:

1. Areas of responsibility are described in the first column. Each area has its own line. All of the activities on that line are executed in the area (most often by the person listed.)

2. Activities are shown in the order of execution. When activities take place concurrently, two or more activity boxes will appear. If one person has the primary responsibility but someone else will also be involved, the secondary action can be shown with a broken line.

3. Events are included on the "results" line. Also on this line are all forms, worksheets, reports, and other documents brought into the project or developed by the team.

4. The time line identifies the time requirement for each activity. In order to track time, you may list each activity's estimated completion on the top of the line and the cumulative estimate on the bottom. An alternative is to list estimated time above, and actual time below. However, plan to keep track of cumulative time as well as to compare estimated to actual.

A network diagram that contains all of these elements will enable you to manage your project without guesswork and without needing to refer to several sources (e.g., a labor estimate *and* a time estimate). All of the information you require for overseeing the project is contained in a single diagram.

When mapped out in this format, your project could run to many pages. For example, a network diagram for a project with twelve areas of responsibility and twenty-five phases broken down into one hundred or more activities will be extremely long. However, the information it provides will be much more useful than what you would have with a simple outline, a vertical flowchart, or a Gantt chart.

The complexity of the project is not a problem; the network diagram is perfectly suited to the most complicated of projects, because your concern at each phase is with keeping work on schedule. In a highly complex project, concurrent activities can become very confusing, and you need a method to track progress in several quarters and at the same time. You won't review the entire network diagram for each phase, but will concentrate only on a small section of it. At the end of each phase, you should ask:

> *Have we completed the activities that need to be completed in order to achieve the event or to proceed to the next activity?*
> *What weak links are we facing or will we be facing in the immediate future?*
> *What actions should we take now to ensure that we stay on schedule?*
> *What results do we need from outside people or departments? Can we make our requests early so that we will have results in hand when we need them?*
> *Are we on schedule? If not, where can we make up the variance?*

Your management efforts will be devoted to a small cross-section of the network diagram. Once you successfully complete a phase, the diagram for the next phase will go into action. When you look over the steps involved, you will be able to quickly spot weak links, heavy activity periods, and results. And the ever-present time line gives you the management tool you need to move a complex project from inception to timely completion.

The diagram is built in steps. You begin with an initial outline, then prepare a vertical flowchart, if necessary. For more complex projects, this might be an important step, if only to ensure that the sequencing of phases makes sense. Then the final network diagram is constructed, with action now moving from left to right instead of from top to bottom. You may undertake this task in several ways:

1. *You can build the network diagram on your own, without the involvement of your team.* Before finalizing it, you may call a meeting and go over the steps, consulting with the group and asking for ideas to improve the schedule.

2. *You may construct the diagram with the whole team involved.* While this might seem like the most participative or democratic approach, it may prove to be the hardest. Committees do not work as efficiently as individuals, and an excessive amount of democracy, at least at the design

stage, could add a lot of time and prevent a final decision. You can still achieve the desired level of participation by working from a sketch of the network diagram and then making changes in response to team ideas.

3. *You may also construct the network diagram with a small group.* For example, if you cannot define all of the activity steps, you will need the involvement of two or three team members. The result can then be presented to the entire team, and adjusted for ideas the group develops. If your team has ten or more members, the small group idea is vastly more practical and efficient than having everyone involved.

APPLYING THE NETWORK DIAGRAM

Using the eight-step project for redesigning procedures first described in Chapter 5 as an example, how should you organize the network diagram? In practice, you will want to list and describe each activity in the boxes so that every team member will be aware of what they and others will be doing. But for the purpose of illustrating how the diagram is constructed, we will describe each of the eight activities by number. And rather than listing out the names or titles of the people in each area of responsibility, we will simply refer to them as *A,B,* and *C.* This project is summarized on the network diagram shown in Figure 7-4.

Several features of this example are worth noting:

1. Weak links are highly visible. They occur between steps 2 and 4, steps 5 and 6, steps 6 and 7, and steps 7 and 8. On the Gantt chart and the vertical flowchart, these many weak links were not identified. Only the network diagram shows you where you are most likely to experience delays.

2. The solid lines are primary activity steps, while the broken lines represent secondary activity. The broken lines and an extra feature you may want to use to make your activity flowchart more practical and still show the primary area of responsibility.

3. Each activity is shown in a box, while each event is listed in the "results" section directly below.

4. Results in this example include the flowchart of current procedures, the new procedures, and the final report. Each of these results from activities that occur directly above.

Figure 7-4. Network diagram application.

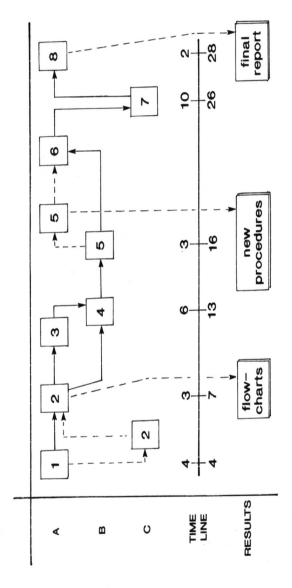

A – AP supervisor

B – accounting manager

C – EDP department

5. The time line shows the time required for each phase (above the line) and the cumulative time for the entire project (below the line). Because several phases take place concurrently, the project should be completed within twenty-eight days.

EXPANDED APPLICATIONS

Our sample project involves a limited team size and a small number of phases. This has been necessary for the purposes of illustration, but many of your projects will involve larger teams, more time, and many more phases.

The network diagram is especially useful when your projects involve documenting procedures, converting systems, and coordinating the efforts of many people or departments. Some examples:

Example 1: You are given the assignment of documenting all of the procedures in your department. The work flow involves interaction between department members as well as with other departments (for information received and for information and reports sent out). A narrative report will be confusing to someone not familiar with your department. And describing each employee's tasks in isolation does not show how the interaction works.

Solution: A network diagram enables you to list each employee on one flowchart. Each person's tasks can be tracked along his or her "area of responsibility" line. And the overall functions can be reviewed together, including identification of weak links, reports and other results, and the time line (tied to your department's monthly processing cycle).

Example 2: Your company is preparing for automation of several departments. Your project is to prepare the documentation that will be needed by the programmers, to identify input formats and fields and the type of information that will be processed, to describe the requirements of the data base, and to define the output desired (e.g., lists or reports).

Solution: The department's processes, when reduced to a network diagram, can be quickly identified and separated into two groups of activity: (1) the recurring routine, which can be easily automated, and (2) the exceptional routine, which may not lend itself to automation. In addition, the network diagram will enable you to estimate input format and data base storage requirements.

Example 3: Your current project is to design a marketing tracking procedure. When it is finalized, several departments will use the procedure: marketing management, field office supervisors, accounting, and marketing and sales support groups.

Solution: To best describe how the procedure you have designed will work, a network diagram does the job. A narrative explanation would not satisfy this need, nor would it clearly show how information is passed from one activity/event cycle to another.

Some projects will require documentation in addition to the network diagram. Because people are not accustomed to such complete visual descriptions of processes, you may need to supplement the schedule with narratives. Or, for certain projects, a network diagram is useful in execution but does not explain exactly what each activity involves or will achieve. This is likely to be the case for projects involving new procedures and conversions.

Chapter 8 shows how narrative sections are used in support of the network diagram, and how you can design the narrative to be the most effective.

WORK PROJECT

1. Explain the difference between an activity and an event in the following cases:
   a. Writing a report
   b. Receiving a report from another department and using it to develop statistical summaries as part of a project phase
   c. Summarizing sales activity information from four separate divisions, and using that information to describe a reporting problem
2. Explain the flaws of vertical flowcharting and how those flaws are overcome by using a network diagram.
3. Why is it essential to identify weak links? How is a network diagram used to ensure continuing schedule control where weak links are involved?

8

Supporting Documentation

If you don't know where you are going, you will probably end up somewhere else.

—Laurence J. Peter

Two project team members, exhausted after a week of working against deadline, were still in the office at 7:30 P.M.

"I'm having trouble following this network diagram," the first one said. "I feel like a rat running through a maze."

"That explains it," the other one replied. "All week, I've had a craving for Cheddar cheese."

How do you manage a project when you have to train your team as you go? Imagine this: You've built a detailed network diagram and tied down all of the loose ends for your project. Your team members know what you expect, but they are confused by the seeming complexity of the diagram itself. Once you get started, you find that several of them still aren't sure *how* you want them to execute their tasks.

The network diagram only identifies the order of execution, shows you where the weak links will occur, and lists what each team member will do and when. But you may need to supply more information to your team. This is especially true when:

1. *Your team includes inexperienced people.* It isn't safe to assume that every project team will always consist of self-starters, or that your team members will be able to do their jobs without supervision. Just as you have to work with your department employees, you have to allot time to work directly with team members, helping them through a task or an entire phase. If that takes away from monitoring, or from phases you planned to execute yourself, you may face a scheduling problem.

2. *The project is exceptionally complicated.* Some projects are technical in nature, but your team may include nontechnical members. Or people assigned to your team because they possess certain skills may not understand how to apply their skills in executing their tasks. In those circumstances, you may need to show your team how these skills should be applied.

3. *You have a very specific idea.* You want to complete your project in a very specific manner to achieve an end result (e.g., a report) that best responds to the assignment. In this case, you need to plan well ahead so that each team member's contribution is aimed at the result you want, and not just executed in the way the team assumes you want it done.

4. *Your team is made up of employees from several departments.* When you work with a team of employees from your department only, you can supervise their efforts daily. However, when several departments are involved, or when your team includes people outside of your company or division, it's not as simple. In this situation, you may need to supply instructions in greater detail to ensure that each phase is completed in the way you want it to be and in coordination with other team efforts.

PROJECT NARRATIVES

When you need to give your team more help than a simple assignment to complete a phase, you will save time and duplication by preparing narrative instructions. These do not need to be extensive—you certainly don't want to write a one-hundred-page training manual. They won't be needed for every step. Supply narrative instructions only where special care is needed or when you want the job done in a specific manner.

You may also need to write instructions for team members who do not understand how to execute a task. Just as employees in your department sometimes need more supervision, project team members cannot always take an assignment and complete it without your help.

Example: One phase of your project involves designing a simplified form. You know your team member is familiar with this, as she has designed forms in the past. Thus, you do not need to write an extensive training narrative for her. However, you might need to list guidelines covering such things as your desire for simplicity, a short list of information you want captured on the form, and a reminder to submit a draft of the form for your approval. These guidelines and procedural steps can be briefly described in narrative form; the step is shown on the network diagram only as "Design a new form."

The narrative section needed for this step can be very brief. For example:

> Design a new form, remembering that we are striving for simplicity. Arrange the information being reported in the same sequence found on source documents. When the first draft is complete, submit it to the project manager for review and approval.

When you work from a network diagram, you should consider the need for narrative support at each step. To reduce the volume of extra material, keep narratives as short as possible, and avoid explaining the obvious points. You should describe processes or provide guidelines only when steps are not self-explanatory or when you expect questions to come up.

Your project team might find brief narratives reassuring as the proceed, especially if they are not used to working from a network diagram. A good many projects are executed haphazardly, with few controls and without the organizational support that a diagram provides. Thus, you may run into resistance to the idea of highly organized processing. Until your team members are trained to think in terms of the overall project and its execution (as expressed on the network diagram), they may have difficulty working from a diagram alone.

Sometimes you may have to describe the entire project even before your team is selected, since you won't know whom you will need for your team until after you've completed a preliminary network diagram and its accompanying instructions. Don't make the mistake of picking a team first and then having to alter the work to fit the people. It makes more sense to select your team members after the diagram and narratives have been prepared so that they can properly execute each phase of the project.

However, the organized approach works well even when your team is chosen before you've broken your project down into phases. For example, you may be given a team to work with, or your department may be given an assignment and expected to function as a team. While this alternative is not as desirable for effective project management, it is unavoidable in many situations.

In such cases, the narrative sections should be written for each team member, not for the overall project or phase. Even though you don't yet have your team together, you still should know what skills you will need to complete the project.

Don't confuse team members by trying to explain too many tasks in one place. Keep the descriptions limited so that only one activity is discussed at any one time, and arrange the narratives in sections tied specifically to each area of responsibility.

Example: You are managing a project to revise procedures in a processing department. During one phase, two different team members will work at the same time in designing a new form. One team member will be responsible for gathering the information that will go on the form, and the other will draft the form itself. Your goal is to write brief narratives explaining how you want the job done. Your first draft reads:

> *Design a new form.*
> Arrange information in the same order found on source documents, using the information supplied by the team member who is gathering information. Remember to strive for simplicity. Submit the draft to the project manager for review.

This may confuse both team members, because the two tasks are described in a single paragraph and different activities are described at the same time. Consider this:

[Redrafted Version]

Design a new form.

Team member 1:
    A: Gathering Information
        Refer to source documents to
        identify the sequence of information.
        List the sequence and submit for
        form design.

Team member 2:
    B: Draft of New Form
        Draft a new form listing
        information in the sequence reported
        above. Strive for simplicity.
    C: Approval
        Submit the draft to the project
        manager for review and approval.

In the redrafted version, the phase is presented in logical sequence. That sequence also distinguishes the steps performed by each of the team members. Each activity is listed as a separate step.

Later in this chapter, you'll learn how to clarify the network diagram by identifying narrative instructions by specific steps and then tying those steps between the narrative and the network diagram. The important point to remember is to keep the narratives clear, short, and helpful.

MORE THAN PAPERWORK

You may begin a project believing that the people on your team are completely capable of executing their tasks without extra training or supervision. But while they may possess the skills that brought them to your team, they may need clarification—especially when the process you have in mind is complicated. This may occur when multiple tasking occurs or when the network diagram has a *loop:* a point where processing may go in more than one direction.

Team members may understand the processing steps if explained clearly, but they may also find the diagram very confusing at this point. That's where the brief narrative helps.

A loop requires a positive or a negative response: correct/incorrect, yes/no, or complete/not complete. Loops occur in several circumstances and can be broken down into three types, as shown in Figure 8-1.

Figure 8-1.   Loops.

VERIFICATION LOOP

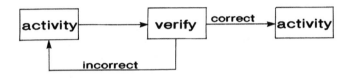

DECISION LOOP

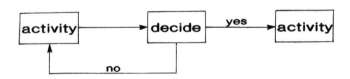

REPETITION LOOP

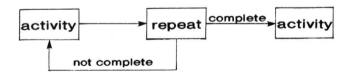

1. *Verification loop.* This occurs where a team member must check information before proceeding. The response is either *correct* or *incorrect.* The balancing of a worksheet is one example. You do not want the team member to proceed until the worksheet has been checked; if a revision is needed, it will be necessary to return to a previous process.

Example: At one point in your network diagram, you indicate the step in the form of a question. The box reads, "Is the balance correct?" Two lines come out of the box. If the answer is "correct," the process moves forward. If the answer is "incorrect," the process moves back to a previous step.

To supplement the network diagram, you prepare a brief narrative of these activities and decisions. It reads:

> *Is the balance correct?*
> Check the balance on the worksheet. If it is correct, move to the next step. If the balance is not correct, return to the previous step; check the numbers transferred to the worksheet, and add once more.

2. *Decision loop.* The decision loop comes up when the process is variable. The response is either *yes* or *no.*

Example: At one step, the team member is asked to find historical information. The question may be, "Is this information adequate to go to the next step?" If the answer is "no," it will be necessary to return and find additional information.

In some cases, the decision will require consultation with someone else.

Example: Upon completion of a rough draft for a new form, the team member submits it to you for approval. If you approve the form, the process can continue. If you want changes, he returns to the design step, makes revisions, and then submits another draft to you.

Your narrative explanation might read:

> *Submit the rough draft for approval.*
> Show the rough draft to the project manager. If the manager approves the design, proceed to the next step. If the manager suggests additional changes, return to the previous step ("Design a new form") and revise. Then return to this step.

3. *Repetition loop.* This loop appears when an activity is repeated more than once. The response is either *complete* or *not complete.*

Example: The step calls for documenting the tasks for each of three people in the department. The activity is applied to each series of tasks, and will be performed three times; thus, a repetition loop is used to explain it.

Your narratives may read:

> *Document tasks.*
> Write brief descriptions of the tasks executed by the first person in the department. Repeat this step for the remaining people. When all task descriptions have been written, proceed to the next step.

If loops confuse your team members, you can clarify the concept by accompanying them with narrative explanations. These narratives are not part of the network diagram but are supplied separately, with one set of narratives for each area of responsibility. So when one person's activities end and someone else's begin, the narrative ends, at least until that person is reactivated.

Your goal is to ensure that each team member has a network diagram and the required narratives for his or her area of responsibility so that tasks can be executed with a minimum level of supervision and a full understanding of what his or her role in the project should be.

SIMPLIFYING INSTRUCTIONS

For some projects, you will need very little in the way of narrative support. But for others you may need to supply team members with a very complete and extensive set of instructions. Base your decision of how much narrative is needed on the people on your team, the degree of complexity of the process, and the number of phases being executed at the same time.

Example: You manage a project with twelve team members. As many phases will be underway at the same time, your network diagram is very complex. In this case, narrative sections will help clarify each member's responsibility, timing, and steps. And because each section of activity begins and ends with weak links (processes moving from one area of responsibility to another), those links are easily identified and planned for in advance.

Example: You manage a project with only a few team members, all of whom also work in your department. There are only a few instances in which phases proceed at the same time. You supply narrative instructions only where the more complex phases are underway.

The purpose of the narratives is to provide more detail than your team members can get from the network diagram. The diagram itself places routines in perspective and helps the team to appreciate the scope of the team effort—even when individual participation in a phase is isolated and seemingly remote from the idea of how "teamwork" proceeds. The network diagram gives the process a visual character. Very seldom will a group of people gather together in a room and truly work together. It's more likely that the team will meet only to decide on the sharing of duties. Then, each person will go away from the meeting and do his or her part.

This environment challenges your leadership abilities. You need to ensure not only that the people on your team share their collective duties and work well together but that each person understands how his or her part fits into the "big picture." The network diagram illustrates this in the best possible way—by showing the critical path process and, at the same time, breaking out each area of responsibility on its own line.

To tie the network diagram to step-by-step narratives, you may want to reproduce the diagram of boxes next to the narratives themselves. This gives you and your team members several benefits:

1. *It makes the flowchart easier to read.* We retain information gained visually better than we do from narratives. The network diagram is visual, as it imposes a pattern on your project and its phases. If the narratives are separate, your team must connect one representation of the task (visual) to other (narrative). Reproducing the boxes next to the narratives overcomes this problem.

2. *It identifies each step directly.* Team members may be intimidated by the complexity and scope of their tasks when reviewed in diagram

form. But when these are broken down and addressed directly as single steps, they will have more confidence in their abilities to respond. Each box is explained, one after the other. This is less overwhelming than the more complex-looking diagram.

   3. *It reverts to vertical steps.* People are accustomed to thinking of processes as moving from top to bottom, as in a vertical flowchart. We've already demonstrated that this method is inefficient for project management, especially since vertical flowcharting fails to show areas of responsibility, time deadlines, or documents generated by project activities. Combining narratives with reproductions of each step (box) gives team members a vertical summary of their tasks.

THE DIAGRAM/NARRATIVE COMBINATION

The complex network diagram can be translated into a fairly simple series of steps, divided into specific areas of responsibility. This improves your team's comprehension, and summarizes each member's individual task and role on the team.

Example: One phase in your project is entitled, "Prepare worksheet." This phase includes a verification loop and, on the diagram, it appears quite complex. The steps on the diagram are depicted as follows:

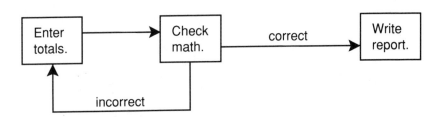

Anticipating that your team member will find this series of steps confusing, you write narrative explanations of the process. To help in tracking the steps, you also reproduce the boxes next to the narrative explanation. The narrative explanation is given to the employee, together with the complete network diagram, as follows:

Refer to the report submitted by the accounting department. This lists the totals of estimated transactions processed by the five processing departments in our division.

Enter the totals from the accounting department report on the worksheet you are preparing. The information you enter should correspond with the column headings you wrote in previously.

When you have completed that step, check the math for each column and for each row. Make certain the worksheet is in balance.

If the worksheet is *not* in balance, return to the previous step. Check each number against the accounting report. Locate all errors and correct the worksheet. Check math once again.

When the worksheet is in balance, proceed to the next step.

Write the report that summarizes the information entered on the worksheet. Submit the report to the project manager for review. Include the worksheet with the report so that the manager will be able to verify the information.

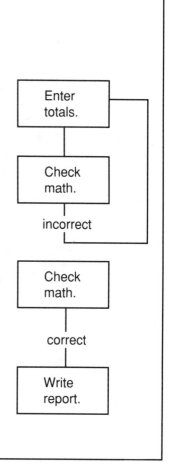

Notice how the horizontal steps on the network diagram are duplicated vertically in the narrative section. Your team members may relate to this step-by-step method more readily than to a complex network diagram. While the diagram is essential to both you and your team, the narrative section—with reproduced steps in boxes—may be the most practical working document for executing project phases efficiently.

Notice that the treatment of the loop is easy to follow. In the diagram, the loop may be the most confusing part, because the process line splits into two directions. With the narrative/diagram combination, this decision is clarified for the team member.

The narrative section is also useful for drawing weak links to your team's attention. Since you will prepare a narrative for each team member, sections will begin and end at natural weak links. One person's involvement begins as someone else completes his or her work, and it ends when the results are passed on to someone else.

In the example given, the team member begins upon receipt of a report from the accounting department. And when the worksheet has been prepared and a subsequent report is written, that work is passed on to the project manager. The beginning and end are the weak links in the project, since work passes from one area of responsibility to another.

The narrative supplement helps every member of your team to manage weak links, because:

1. The process itself cannot begin until the previous work is completed and passed through.
2. The process is not complete until the last step, which often is to pass results on to the next person to execute the next phase.

As project manager you will find it easiest to control the schedule by tracking the time line on the network diagram. This is best managed with a visual summary, since you can view progress of the entire project no matter how many different tasks are underway at one time. However, when a team member runs into a problem, you will find the narrative section very helpful for working through the problem and arriving at a solution.

PROJECT CONTROL DOCUMENTATION

Because every project is different, no one level of documentation will be appropriate in every case. The level should be dictated by the need. In some cases you may want a very formal, elaborate series of documents that not only show the progress of activity but also define areas of responsibility. This may help to avoid overlap in execution, especially when your project team is spread out over several departments and includes a large number of people.

In that instance, the overall documentation you prepare is similar to the specifications an engineer draws up before building a structure. Several definitions are required in the larger project: who will take charge of each phase, the scope of their responsibilities, the materials they will need, and the appearance of the end result.

You face a similar task when you manage a long-term project with a large project team. Here, each phase should be broken down according to the individual team member having primary responsibility and, if necessary, according to those who will participate in secondary roles. The schedule should be broken down and illustrated by way of needed detail, which may include an outline, a Gantt chart, and a PERT/CPM network. You may also need a network diagram so that you can control progress and stay on schedule while working with a number of team members during various phases. For some projects, development of the network diagram is possible only as a series of definitions, arrived at by making up first an outline, then a Gantt chart, then a PERT/CPM, and, finally, a network diagram that incorporates all of the scheduling and timing issues resolved in previous steps.

The complex project—one that demands many months and a large project team—will be better defined and controlled when narratives are thorough enough to show each team member what is involved in his or her area of responsibility, often with a good amount of detail.

Example: Your project is to devise procedures for a department currently processing transactions manually. The company plans to automate the department within the next six months, and your project will achieve several end results:

- Definition of required data base size, including an estimate of the number of transactions processed per month.
- Procedures for input, verification, and documentation of work
- Design of input and control forms
- Design of data base elements
- Design of several reports to be drawn from the data base for various purposes

- Procedures for training employees in the use of the revised methods of work in the department

Team members for this project will include a number of people from the department being automated, some from your own department, and some from data processing. In addition, you will work with outside consultants who have been hired to assist your companay in tailoring existing programs and writing new routines.

Therefore, you need an extensive series of narratives on several levels:

- Instructions to your project team for gathering and summarizing information
- Methods of drafting initial results and then submitting them for approval
- Guidelines for writing new procedures, designing forms, and communicating with data processing technical and support staff

Because the project involves many team members who work in a number of different departments (and outside of the company), it's important to define areas of responsibility before getting started. This should be one of the first sections of your project documentation book.

You define areas of responsibility for this project in three ways:

1. *Type of work.* An employee in your department will be responsible for drafting the data base files for the new system, in coordination with a data processing consultant. Another employee from your department is given the series of tasks related to the design of forms.

2. *Individuals who, by virtue of their jobs, have special knowledge or skills.* Data processing department employees will be responsible for the efforts resulting in applications of the new system.

3. *Phases of the project.* A phase, by its nature, may dictate which individuals on your team should be placed in charge. When several departments or people are involved, one individual should be given primary responsibility, and everyone else involved should agree to that decision. Without this definition, you may have problems getting various members to perform as a team.

The documentation file you create, whether very limited or very detailed and extensive, will help you to monitor your project and stay on schedule. Hopefully, it will also define areas of responsibility well enough so that every member of your team knows exactly what you expect, when it must be completed, and how to proceed.

With the proper documentation—notably the combination of network diagram and required narratives—you have the tools to successfully lead your project team toward timely completion. To achieve this, you will need to develop methods for periodic review, including progress reporting, deadline control, and actions designed to make up delays and absorb budget variances. Project review is the subject of Chapter 9.

WORK PROJECT

1. You are writing narrative instructions for a project phase involving two team members and a decision step. The sequence of activities is:
   a. Team member 1 prepares an outline of tasks, and gives the outline to team member 2.
   b. Team member 2 reviews the outline. If he has any questions, he meets with team member 1, and asks for more information.
   c. Once team member 2 has the information needed, he prepares a step-by-step flowchart of the procedures.
   How would you combine narratives with activity and decision boxes to describe these steps for each of the two team members?
2. Describe the typical features of:
   a. Verification loops
   b. Decision loops
   c. Repetition loops
3. Describe and explain three ways that areas of responsibility are defined in a project narrative document.

9
Project Review

There is a point where we have to say that enough is enough and we have to start the implementation.

—Dennis Hayes

"I think there's too much bureaucracy in this company," one manager confided to another. "Last month, the president formed a task force to figure out why projects weren't being finished on schedule."

"I know. It struck me as a good idea," the other manager replied.

"Except for one thing. They haven't submitted their report yet, and it was due three weeks ago."

One very successful project manager identified the reason she never went over budget or missed a deadline: constant review and monitoring. Never satisfied with a plan as originally conceived, she spent at least as much time following the team's progress as she spent involved in the work itself.

Your role should be to keep your team working toward the final deadline, within the budget, and in line with the objective of the project. This effort may demand more time than you spend actually working on phases of the project.

THE PROGRESS REVIEW

It might appear that a "successful" project is one that is completed on time, and within budget. In fact, though, these surface achievements are most likely to be realized when the people on your team have a sense of satisfaction from their efforts. In some cases, the real problems leading to budget and schedule failures are not merely mechanical or chance events but other problems your team is encountering.

You face three problems in the review process:

1. *Defining standards of performance.* What do you expect from your team? The obvious answers—meeting phase and project deadlines and staying within the project budget—are constant concerns. But beyond these issues are questions of quality, cooperation, and results. Thus, your review should also consist of checking for accuracy and thoroughness, for achievement of a teamwork ideal, and for comprehensive and correct interpretation of raw data.

2. *Finding appropriate applications of the standards.* As your project moves foward, how do you test the standards you have set, and what does your test reveal? This is where many project reviews fall short. You may work with your team in the definition stages of the project, carefully pinpointing the desired results to be achieved. However, you also need a method for determining whether the standards are being met.

3. *Deciding what actions, if any, you need to take.* What should you do upon discovering problems? Your team may be falling behind schedule, for example. That's a problem in itself, but it may also be a symptom of a deeper team problem. Getting back on schedule may not be as difficult a task as solving the underlying problem—whether the issue is teamwork, ability, communication, effort, authority, or motivation. Identifying the underlying problem and then taking action to solve it are two areas where your leadership will be severely tested.

With these problems in mind, you should be able to determine whether your team is following the standards you have agreed upon and whether you are on schedule and within budget. Beyond that, you also need to ensure that the project team is, indeed, working as a team. Is one key person doing all of the work while the rest of the team does nothing?

Or are team members failing in what you consider cooperative effort by not working well together? There are any number of ways that team-related problems can lead to obvious scheduling and budgeting problems.

Your standards will vary according to the nature of the project. If a large part of the work involves research—the accumulation of information, compiling, interpreting, and reporting—your standards should include absolute accuracy and attention to detail. If the project will conclude with a report to management, you will want to ensure that the information is arranged, indexed, and referenced properly. Each project's characteristics point the way to identifying the most likely standards.

In addition to standards for executing the project itself, you will want to apply your own personal standards—your definition of "excellence." Since the team's efforts will at least partially reflect on your ability to lead, you must be very concerned with the impression your team creates.

How frequently should you review your team's progress? Some managers consider review to be a formal, exceptional procedure, as in an employee's job performance evaluation that takes place once or twice a year. Others make review an ongoing, constant effort; in every effort and contact, the review question is on their minds.

No matter what theory you subscribe to as a departmental manager, as project manager you should take the second, ongoing approach. Review cannot be performed periodically, because problems may arise too suddenly, and become irreversible too quickly if you are not continually looking for them. The best project managers are always at least one step ahead of difficulties, solving them before they are allowed to get out of hand and destroy the course of successful completion.

Remember, too, that projects deal in exceptions rather than routines. In your department, you expect each employee to handle a range of duties; definition of the job is usually very clear. In projects, though, team members are asked to execute a range of tasks for which they are qualified but in contexts that are often foreign to them. Thus, you may have to be more involved in training your team than you are in training employees executing activities in your department.

As a method and approach, constant review is more likely to ensure success than the periodic review. Waiting until a problem comes to your attention may mean that you're taking too passive a role, especially when projects are executed over a relatively short time span, as most are. By the time you realize the deadline won't be met, it may already be too late.

MONITORING AND REPORTING

You will report progress on two levels: first, to the team, as an opportunity to acknowledge effort and motivate individuals, to identify emerging problems and propose solutions, and to anticipate and prevent upcoming difficulties; second, to management, either to the person who gave you the project assignment or to a group of executives who are interested in the results of your team effort.

Report to the Team

Your report to the team is a form of performance review. Since you expect the individuals to work together under your leadership, it also makes sense to make your report to the entire group, and at one time. The review process itself may be ongoing, but the report is made during periodic team meetings.

These meetings, which may be scheduled periodically during the project's time span, should take place at critical points—immediately before or after a key phase, for example. Large, complex projects may lend themselves to a number of report/review meetings; projects with smaller, shorter time spans may require only one or two. Although these meetings should take as much time as is required to communicate your message and to take feedback from the team, as a rule, they should be extremely short. If you are working with a large team on a number of concurrent activities, you may need to include the meeting process as part of the schedule itself—as actual phases of the project—rather than merely call the team together from time to time.

Report to Management

Your report to management is likely to be more formal but less detailed. Here your concern is not with the details of execution but with whether the project will be completed on time and within budget. Any problems meeting those requirements should be discussed in the management progress report.

Even though your company may not require a progress report from you, it might be wise to suggest such a policy, notably for longer-term projects with large budgets that involve a large number of employees (e.g., a one-year project to automate several processes, demanding a team of twenty-five employees, consultants, and departments, not to mention a budget in six figures). In situations like this, budget and schedule reviews are essential—not to mention the need to assure yourself that your efforts are aimed toward the right objectives.

If your company does expect a progress report, it should probably be prepared in written form, even if you deliver the report verbally. Make it a matter of personal policy always to prepare a brief written summary of your presentation. You may also want to insist on written reports from departmental and project team employees, to help them become professional department and project managers of the future.

What should your report contain, and how long should it be? The report to management should convey only the information it needs to know about your project (for example, there is no need to list the details of an earlier delay that was absorbed later). Limit the report to include only the following:

1. A very brief description of the project and its final deadline

2. Current status (schedule and budget)

3. Explanations where needed, especially of time and money variances

4. Expectations for the near future—completion of the project compared to deadline

Both schedule and budget status can be boiled down to one page. For example, you might want to include the budget variance report form, in which only major variances are accompanied by explanations, or a Gantt chart, which gives an excellent summary of your schedule. Don't include the more detailed network diagram used to monitor your team's progress. There is no need to burden management with unnecessary detail.

If your project is on schedule and within budget, the entire report can be as short as three pages—one each for the schedule and the budget, and one to describe the project and add the one and only comment: "This project is on schedule and should be completed on time and within the expense budget."

When further explanation is required, try to identify the problems in terms of likely solutions. What can the person receiving the report do to help you overcome a problem? Anything other than action-oriented comments are not productive.

Example: You are preparing a report on the status of your project. You are currently on schedule, but you expect to run into problems in the coming month. Another department was expected to provide information to you, but the manager of that department recently told you it would be late: She has been given a separate, unexpected, and unscheduled job, and the deadline is critical; she simply doesn't have the staff available to complete the work promised to you. This will delay your final deadline by two weeks.

A critical point to remember concerning your report to management: Missing a promised deadline is not always a disaster (in fact, in some situations, management accepts delays as normal). What is a disaster, though, is failing to disclose the delay in advance. Your report should be as accurate and as complete as possible, even if it contains bad news.

In the example given, there are two ways to disclose the problem. One is to place blame, which does not solve the problem. Another method is to offer constructive solutions where possible. You can state in your explanation, "The project will be delayed by two weeks, because we don't expect Department X to deliver its work on time." Or you can explain, "Based on the current schedule, the project will be delayed by two weeks. We recommend that Department X be given additional temporary help so that it may deliver its report according to schedule."

Under the second alternative, you propose a solution to the problem without placing blame. Chances are, the other manager can do nothing to solve the delay problem, and who's to blame is of no interest to the person reading your report. Proposed solutions are far more revealing about the character of the project—and of the project manager.

THE MISSED DEADLINE

You may speculate on the question of deadlines and conclude that management is not terribly concerned with timely completion. This is the unfortunate state of affairs in many companies: Deadlines are missed so often that missed deadlines become normal.

I suggest that you take every deadline seriously as a promise to deliver, and consider that delay is not acceptable unless it's also unavoidable. If it is, then management should be advised as early as possible that the deadline will not be kept.

Remember these important points concerning deadlines:

1. *They may be set early on purpose.* If your company's management is accustomed to missed deadlines, it may fall into the habit of imposing an early deadline—in the hopes that you will finish your project by the time they really need it. For example, the president must have your report no later than May 1; you are given a final deadline of April 1, in the belief that the extra four weeks will be enough time to complete the job.

Setting early deadlines only encourages continuing failure to meet them; thus, the problem is intensified rather than solved. The best way to overcome this situation is to meet the early deadline whenever possible.

2. *Management may accept missed deadlines.* Top management may not be happy about the fact that deadlines are often missed, but it may live with the situation because "everyone does it." This is not an acceptable solution to the overall problem, and it should never be used as a reason for missing the deadline on your project—under any circumstances whatsoever.

3. *Management may depend on your timely delivery to decide on other matters.* To a project manager deeply involved in the details of keeping a project on schedule, the immediate deadline may seem like the highest priority. Remember, though, management may be waiting on the results of your project to decide other matters. If you miss your deadline, the consequences may be more far-reaching than just your project.

4. *One of your responsibilities is keeping management in touch with your work.* As project manager, you are charged with the duty of letting management know what's going on—just as you are accountable for budgets, schedules, and results in your capacity as a department manager. Missed deadlines and emerging problems (with proposed solutions) should be conveyed upwards. The pipeline from you to top management should be open and consistent; hopefully information will flow in both directions.

5. *Delays may be acceptable, not because they happen frequently, but because of other delays beyond your project.* Management may express little concern when you advise them that your project will be late. Don't assume that this means your missed deadline is not a problem. It may be that other delays have made your original deadline less critical.

Example: You have been given the project of proposing new budget guidelines. Your final report, you realize, will be six weeks late. When you inform management, their response is, "No problem." You don't know, however, that management wanted your report as part of a companywide revision and that the larger project has been delayed for three months.

6. *You can ask for an extension.* Some project managers fear telling management that their projects won't be completed on time, so they take the worst possible course: saying nothing. When you're under pressure to complete a number of phases and meet a final deadline, it's easy to overlook the fact that you *can* ask for an extension, and that it might be granted. This is far better than just letting the matter drop and not communicating with management at all.

7. *You might overcome delays by looking for shortcuts.* Upon review, you may conclude that the deadline will be missed because you've dropped behind schedule. But that's not always the case. You may be able to make up the lost time by taking shortcuts between now and the final deadline. For example, some phases may be executed in a shorter time span than you've allowed. Perhaps you've built a time cushion into the later phases and can now take advantage of it.

A word of caution concerning shortcuts: Be sure they save time without also shorting the results or the quality of your team's effort. It's better to be late than to finish up with inaccurate results that don't fulfill your original objective.

ACCELERATING THE SCHEDULE

Here's a problem you will run into time and again: The project is proceeding efficiently, right on schedule, and with no signs of a delay. Then, a single problem (such as finding out that completion of one phase is more complex than you estimated) throws your whole schedule into disarray.

Being able to anticipate problems of this nature is a matter of experience. The more time you spend managing projects, the better able you will be to identify areas where "unexpected" delays will occur. Perhaps they're most likely where several weak links occur together, where you depend on an outside department or consultant, or where several efforts merge together for the final push to the deadline.

Even the most experienced project manager will run into problems, however, and dealing with the unexpected and sudden delay requires skill and fast action. You may be able to anticipate and plan for the delay if today's project runs a course similar to others you have managed and when you know where the problems are likely to occur. But that doesn't guarantee that every project will be entirely predictable. On the contrary, one of the challenging aspects of managing projects is that each one takes on a character of its own.

You may not always be able to depend on acceleration as a solution to delay. Even when you build slack time into the later phases, delays sometimes quickly outrun the two or three days you've allowed. Deadlines often impose a tight scheduling demand on projects, and you may have very little flexibility toward the end of the project term. However, by increasing efficiency and teamwork, you may still be able to absorb a serious delay in one of the later phases.

The problem is not as easily solved when delays are caused in areas of responsibility outside your direct control. Sometimes, when your project team consists not only of people from your own department but of consultants and people from other departments and divisions, you can't enjoy the same kind of hands-on control that you do within your own department.

Example: Your schedule is delayed because one phase turns out to be more time-consuming than you expected, so you assign a team member from your department to work on another phase exclusively. At the same time, you shift his departmental work to other employees.

Example: You cannot enter your final phase until you receive a report from another department, but due to an unexpectedly heavy workload, the manager of that department has been forced to put your work aside. Unless you can supply relief by lending employees to the other manager, there's nothing you can do to fix this problem.

In addition to being limited in terms of resources and time, you may not be able to overcome certain political problems: another manager may resist your offer of help, or even feel pressured if you make the offer. She may also react negatively to any suggestion that will help her to meet *your* deadline. Thus, whenever dealing with delays caused by outside resources or team members, you need to remain aware of the potential political problems your offer of help could cause.

THE CHANGING OBJECTIVE

One of the most frustrating experiences a project manager can suffer is having a project's nature changed—while it's underway. It may seem illogical to think that management would alter an assignment *after* allowing you to invest your team's effort in many weeks or months of endeavor. However, a project's objective and end result may change for a number of reasons.

The ever-changing climate of your company may cause an effort to become obsolete very rapidly—due to economic, competitive, and capital considerations, for example. A change in top management may be accompanied by a change in priorities, and even in the direction of expansion and other efforts. A new CEO's philosophy could render a project meaningless within his first few hours in office.

Even without the influence of change, management may waver in their own course. While this is disruptive and dangerous for morale, you have no control over its occurrence. In companies that are led by people with no strong sense of purpose, indecision can mark the whole corporate culture. The people who suffer from this problem are, of course, the workers and their managers, on both the departmental and project level.

There is little to be said for arguing in favor of keeping an original objective. Resisting the change only marks you as a troublemaker and does little for the reputation you want to encourage—that you are a member of the "team" as management defines it. A more positive approach will save a lot of time and energy.

Your response should include these steps:

1. *Immediately inform the team.* Avoid adopting an antimanagement attitude when your project's objective—or its very life—is threatened. Explain why the change is occurring, and then make the best of it.
2. *Concentrate on executing the change, rather than on less productive and more negative activities.* Do everything you can to channel your team's energy into the new effort.
3. *Revise your schedule and budget.* If you need to make substantial changes (e.g., delay the project's deadline), write a brief report and submit it for approval.
4. *Revise your control forms,* especially those concerned with schedule control (e.g., PERT/CPM, network diagram, Gantt chart).

You will be able to avoid the majority of changed objectives by asking for clear definition before you begin work on your project. Most changes result not from outside influences beyond your company's control but from lack of definition—a problem that often is found at the top of the company. But although it is management's job to define, you may have to force definition from an executive who falls short of that responsibility.

When the executive resists your efforts at defining the project, chances are greater that (1) the course will be changed midway or (2) he or she won't be happy with the outcome. Thus, the more effort you put into asking for definition at the beginning, the lower the chances that your team's efforts will be wasted.

STAYING ON COURSE

Successful project review can be accomplished only if the project's objectives remain unchanged. Once a project is given a revised definition, your judgment needs to be revised as well. When you begin your project, you will assume that it will continue through to the successful completion of a stated objective. That requires guidelines, which not only set standards for your team but provide you with a course of review.

Your guidelines should include these points:

1. *Make sure that everyone on your team has a specific range of duties (an area of responsibility), and that relationships between team members are clearly defined.* With this level of definition, your team will be able to work together and avoid the conflicts and uncertainties found in ill-defined projects.

2. *Do not restrict your tests of successful progress only to questions of scheduling and budgets.* You will also look for signs of team conflict and be prepared to step in and mediate a solution.

3. *Test what you can control.* Problems created by outside influences cannot be solved by any action you take. Thus, testing for them is useful only to the extent that you can anticipate them.

4. *Tackle the project with an action orientation.* Take steps to solve short-term problems, while keeping an eye on the final deadline. And instruct your team to communicate with you, especially when they expect problems in upcoming phases of the project.

5. *Support your team.* Review their work, but remember that the success of the project also depends on your being available when your team needs you, how much help you supply in getting through difficult phases, and how willing you are to back up a team member when he or she confronts a problem with an outside resource.

The success of your project and, to a greater extent, the sense of success your team gains by working with you depend on how well you communicate. In addition to monitoring and reviewing the project, you need to ensure that the lines of communication remain open—between you and the team as well as between the team and outside resources or members. That's the topic of Chapter 10.

WORK PROJECT

1. Describe the three problems you face in reviewing a project, and tell how solving each one improves the review process.
2. Why is it important to review your team's progress continually? Compare project and department reviews.
3. What four elements should you include in a review report to management, for ongoing projects?

10

The Communication Challenge

Make no little plans: they have no magic to stir men's blood. . . . Make big plans, aim high in hope and work.

—David H. Burnham

A manager received a memo through the interoffice mail. It read in part, "We must keep the lines of communication open between our departments in order to ensure the success of this project. Please call me as soon as possible so that we can discuss schedules and deadlines."

The manager told his assistant, "I'd like to answer, but whoever wrote this memo forgot to sign it."

We've all heard the clichés about communication. But putting the ideas into practice is often a lot harder than applying the theories. This is even truer for project management than for departmental management.

While managing your department, you're in constant contact with your staff. Their tasks are well-defined and recurring. Your people are focused on performance, and their careers depend on how well they execute their tasks. A project, by comparison, is often seen as an intrusion, a departure from the normal routine—even when it's "normal" to disrupt that routine with a series of projects.

In addition to the manager-team dynamics, you must contend with communication on three other levels:

1. *The assignment.* The executive (or committee) that first assigned the project to you may not agree with your idea of what the project should achieve; or he may change his mind about the outcome without letting you know.
2. *Other departments.* The managers of other departments have their own priorities and may resist your schedule. This usually applies in two situations: when members of their department are on your team or when you depend on that department to supply certain information.
3. *Outside resources.* Your project may depend on help or information from "outside" resources—companies or individuals not part of the organization. These include other divisions, subsidiaries, or offices; a vendor or separate corporation; or a consultant.

Your budget and schedule are your best communication tools. They are useful in communicating with both your team members and outside resources. Each can be used in a number of ways.

THE BUDGET AS A COMMUNICATION TOOL

The budget defines the company's financial commitment, and is used to ensure that project expenses are kept in line. If variances do occur, they often anticipate a scheduling problem as well.

The budget also measures the degree of risk involved with your project. Any change in the company is accompanied by risk, and when time and money are spent, the decision to go ahead is based on a judgment of risk. Management will proceed with the project if it is convinced that the risk is acceptable and that future profit potential justifies that risk. So, for example, when you propose a project, you should *communicate* in terms of risk and likely reward. Approval will be granted as long as you can convince management that there's a good chance that future profits will recapture this investment within a reasonable period of time.

THE SCHEDULE AS A COMMUNICATION TOOL

The schedule defines the project, and, as long as you share it with management, it is a useful tool for ensuring that your definition conforms to theirs. When it's broken down into phases, with deadlines tied to the final result, management has the opportunity to validate your direction, and you can ensure that your understanding of the project's goals is correct. At this early stage, you can define exactly what the project should achieve.

You also need to use the schedule during the later phases of your project in conjunction with review meetings to ensure (1) that you are on the right course and (2) that management's desired outcome has not changed.

Finally, the schedule improves communication with your team, and helps avoid delays. By identifying weak links and by communicating with other department managers and outside resources, you will avoid unexpected problems.

WORKING WITH OTHER DEPARTMENT MANAGERS

For relatively simple short-term projects that are executed strictly within a single department, you, as department manager, have direct control over the time commitments and priorities of each team member. Because you are aware of your department's deadlines and workload variations, you can build your schedule around the workload and adjust it as needed. You can also balance departmental and project demands on the basis of your knowledge of each and the scheduling flexibility and control you're able to exercise.

As the scope of your project grows, your task assumes a greater dimension, and you will begin to work with people from other departments. This is where your communication skills are tested.

A common complaint often heard from other managers is, "You didn't tell me in time," regardless of whether problems arise because of deadlines, the use of an employee's time, or conflicts in commitment. But you can solve most of the problems you will encounter in working with other departments by remembering this key point:

*Keep other department managers informed at all times: before
and during the project.*

By applying a few basic rules for communication between departments, you will be able to defuse the problems that beset all managers at
one time or another: territorial motives, power struggles, and—in cases
where communication breaks down completely—outright refusal to
cooperate. Most of the time, the breakdown of cooperation arises not
from a political or personality problem but from a failure in the communication link—especially when you have made the effort to communicate, but only once. People need periodic reminding, so don't assume
that a single message will be remembered.

Figure 10-1 summarizes the following rules for improving and
maintaining your communication with other departments.

1. *Visit the other manager before you finalize the schedule.* From your
point of view, it might seem that a given schedule has to go into effect.
For example, the deadline allows little room for change, and an employee
from another department has been placed on your team by the company
president. So why contact the team member's supervisor? Everything
has been settled.

Because no matter how restricted you are by the deadline, and no
matter how little say you have been given in picking your team, you

Figure 10-1.   Outside department checklist.

1. **Visit the other manager before
   you finalize the schedule.**

2. **Keep in touch while the project
   is underway.**

3. **Work with the manager to
   anticipate problems.**

4. **Remain as flexible as possible.**

5. **Confront the problems, not the
   people.**

must be prepared to make changes to accommodate the other manager. Plan to discuss the employee's involvement well before you finish your schedule. Take this approach: Ask for a meeting with the other manager; present your initial schedule, explaining that it is only preliminary; and state clearly that the purpose of the meeting is to determine whether your schedule will present any problems in that other department.

2. *Keep in touch while the project is underway.* Continue to keep the lines of communication open. Even when the manager has agreed to your schedule, unexpected scheduling conflicts can and do come up later.

You can avoid conflict by keeping in touch with the manager throughout the project period. A weekly status check may be all that's required. In a three-minute telephone discussion, you can go over the team member's commitments for the week, ensuring that there are no problems. If the other manager is given an unexpected, perhaps separate, project, that assignment could create tremendous problems for both of you. By working together, you will be able to resolve them, but if you don't stay in touch, the difficulty could grow into a serious conflict in priorities.

3. *Work with the manager to anticipate problems.* In addition to the review, look to the end of your project. Point out the phases that will require an especially heavy time commitment, and ask the other manager, "Do you expect this to create a problem in your department?"

Most managers will appreciate your consideration, and will glady work with you to resolve any upcoming difficulties. It's only when you don't anticipate future problems that conflict arises, obscuring your priorities and jeopardizing the relationship between you and the other manager.

4. *Remain as flexible as possible.* Remember that few departments can judge very far in advance the demands that will be placed on them from above. It's frustrating when another manager affects your scheduling by pulling a team member out of a commitment in order to work on other jobs. This is not necessarily because he or she is devious or disorganized. It may simply characterize that department.

Stop and think whenever you find yourself about to say, "You told me this wouldn't be a problem." At the time, the manager was probably telling you the truth. But since then, the department's assignments, deadlines, and priorities have changed. Successful project managers are those who are able to stay on schedule and within budget, even when team members are taken away at the last minute. You may have to shift jobs or take over a phase yourself. Regardless of the inconvenience, though, remain flexible when dealing with another manager.

   5. *Confront the problems, not the people.* In some instances, other managers may seem unreasonable, defensive, or uncooperative; they may feel threatened by having an employee taken away from them to work on your project.

   Territorial reaction is one form of "corporate neurosis." Your refusal to tolerate it won't solve the problem. Nor will confronting the manager directly; that only aggravates the situation. Remember, the best solution is to concentrate on the problem the reaction creates, not to become distracted by the personal reaction itself.

   When a manager resists your efforts to commit an employee, emphasize the schedule and deadline. Ask the manager to suggest a solution that satisfies the departmental needs as well as the project schedule. Avoid the distraction of arguing about personal priorities, and concentrate on executing the task.

WORKING WITH OTHER DEPARTMENT EMPLOYEES

The communication challenge is not limited just to managers. You may also face resistance from team members. Conflicts can arise for a number of reasons:

1. *Career priorities.* Some employees identify their career paths with their departments, not with outside projects. They can't always appreciate the career advancement potential that comes from taking part in projects, especially those managed by people other than their immediate supervisors.
2. *Temporary assignments.* Because it's temporary, your project may be seen as an inconvenient disruption, as extra work. So some employees may assume a different attitude toward project tasks than they do toward their "real" jobs.

3. *Supervisory problems*. As manager of a project, you do not determine the quality of corporate life to the same degree an immediate supervisor does, and once the project is over, your team
members return to their departments.

To overcome these problems, apply the same rules you use in
dealing with managers of other departments. Be aware of the team
members' priorities and conflicts. As long as they are working on your
project, they're in the difficult position of reporting to two people. Do
all that you can to alleviate this problem, rather than aggravate it.

Remember, your team members have to meet deadlines on two
levels: those of their own department and those of your project. Work
with them to solve conflicts in schedules and to anticipate future problem
periods.

Once you discover an emerging problem, take immediate steps to
solve it. Never assume the attitude that "you're part of my team; I
depend on you, and you have to keep your promise." Instead, sit down
with the team member and figure out a solution. Either reassign the
project phase or adjust your schedule.

The project schedule is *your* problem and *your* responsibility. So
even when a team member cannot come through as promised, it's up to
you to do something about it. You can create a positive reputation as a
project manager by establishing two-way loyalty: from the team by their
working together and meeting deadlines, and to the team by your
remaining flexible, especially when a team member cannot keep a
promise to you.

Since project leadership is limited when you work with employees
from other departments, you need to change your leadership style. If
you are used to supervising people only on the departmental level, you
could run into problems applying the same standards—and expecting
the same response—from team members who do not report to you
directly. This situation requires you directly. This situation requires
supervision on a level quite different from what you use in your
department.

It may take considerable thought to choose the style that works best
for your project, and it will vary. It all depends on the attitude of the
other department manager, the clarity with which top management has

communicated the project's goals to everyone, and the length and time commitment of the project itself.

WORKING WITH OUTSIDE CONSULTANTS

Your communications skills may be severely tested when your team includes a consultant. You need to contend not only with the independence of the outside adviser but also with the question of who is running the project.

Consultants are oriented toward projects; many even function as project managers. In fact, the most sensible arrangement is to retain consultants only for management of carefully defined projects. However, this may lead to problems for you as the inside manager.

Example: One manager was given a project where she had to work with an outside consultant. From the first day, it was apparent that the consultant viewed his role as that of project manager. When the project manager met with the vice president who had assigned the project, she discovered that she'd been given the assignment primarily to act as liaison between the consultant and the company; in fact, her role was subordinate to the consultant's and she was *not* truly the project manager.

While this may be an example of poor communication at the top, it also demonstrates the way consultants are often brought into a company. Management may feel compelled to assign responsibility for a project within the company, but the real authority belongs to the consultant. This can create terrible friction and conflict unless you define the relationship and chain of command at the beginning of your project.

Another situation involves the independence of the consultant. Chances are, he or she has many other clients and will not be able to give a large amount of time to your project. Even when the consultant understands that you are the manager, you may have a problem in scheduling his or her time commitment. Your deadline, as critical as it is to you, may not be met if the consultant delays his or her participation.

Therefore, make sure that your schedule is not entirely dependent on the consultant's work. If you have critical tasks that must be performed by the consultant before a subsequent phase can be entered, and if the consultant is late, the entire project will be delayed. Even though you are responsible for meeting the deadline, the resulting delay may be beyond your control. You can deal with this problem in several ways:

1. *Design your schedule so that the consultant's task is given an early deadline.* Whenever possible, ask for the work from the consultant far in advance of the critical date. This is not always practical, since his or her work may depend on first completing a previous phase. But as a general rule, any work that does not depend on other completion (whether performed by outside consultants or inside team members) should be scheduled as early as possible.

2. *Be prepared to complete the work without the consultant.* In some cases, you can execute the phase management expects from the consultant yourself. The consultant may have been hired because management thinks he or she has superior ability or knowledge, but if that isn't necessarily the case, you can work around the consultant by reassigning work to other team members. However, whenever this occurs, be sure to report the change in assignment to management.

3. *Accept the delay as being beyond your control.* In many cases, you will not be able to work around the consultant, so you will simply have to accept the delay—not only of the one phase but, as a consequence, of the entire project. Once you realize that you cannot meet the deadline, inform management at once.

Your experience with outside consultants will not always be negative. In a large number or projects and other corporate endeavors, consultants play an important and valuable role. Just remember that you do not have the same degree of supervisory control as when you work with inside employees. The consultant, by nature, has a point of view outside of the corporate chain of command.

WEAK LINKS IN COMMUNICATION

We previously explained weak links in scheduling and execution of tasks. Whenever work passes from one person or department to another, the opportunity for delay or misunderstanding is present. By knowing where the weak links exist, you will be able to ensure that the project moves forward, on track, and on schedule.

You will encounter a communication weak link whenever you deal with someone else, and whenever your team members explain, discuss, or speak to another person. In other words, effective communication itself is the solution to the identification and elimination of weak links. The weak links include:

1. *Manager to team member.* Whenever you speak to a team member, you encounter a weak link. For example, you instruct a team member to "get the historical information and summarize it on a worksheet." Unless you can clarify exactly what you want, the work may not be performed in the way you expect. What historical information? How should it be summarized? What will the worksheet look like?

If you don't communicate clearly, chances are the work will have to be revised. And whenever that happens, the team member will complain that your instructions were vague. Thus, make sure that your instructions are absolutely clear, that you explain exactly what you want, and—most of all—that the team member understands exactly what you expect.

2. *Manager to outside department manager.* Your second weak link occurs when the manager of another department is involved—either as a resource for your project or as someone a team member reports to. The more clearly you explain the scope of the project and the time it will require, the better your chances for full cooperation. The other manager has a point of view you need to respect and understand. For example, the project may make his or her job more complicated, as it takes a resource away from the department. An outside department employee might view your project as extra work, while the other manager may see it as a strain on a limited staff.

The solution: Respect other managers' problems and conflicts. Recognize that their priorities are not the same as yours. Although your project may demand you time and effort even more than the work in your department, that isn't necessarily the case for other managers.

3. *Manager to outside resource.* No matter how urgent your deadlines or how important the project is to the company, you may have difficulty getting response from an outside resource—a consultant, a vendor, or another division. Their priorities are simply not the same as yours.

Thus, the potential weak link is a considerable one. *The solution:* anticipate problems in the way you schedule, in the timing of your requests, and in the way you keep in touch. Don't wait until the deadline is upon you, but plan well ahead to eliminate the problem through communicating as clearly as possible.

4. *Manager to executive.* Once you are given a project, your first task should be to ensure that you and management are in complete agreement. What is the purpose and the desired end result? You may execute a project according to the highest standards and come in on schedule and within budget. But if the result is not what the executive wanted, your efforts will have been wasted. You need to define your processes and your schedule, and check with the person who gave you the assignment.

Another problem may arise when the executive changes the assignment. This may occur without your knowledge. For example, a decision is made at the board level, and the executive's priorities change, but you are not informed of this decision. Anticipating that this could occur, you need to make periodic reports while your project is underway. It's the executive's responsibility to draw your attention to a wrong direction, but this may occur only if you make the effort to reaffirm the way you are executing the assignment.

HOW FLOWCHARTING HELPS

The communication challenge exists on many levels and stays with you throughout the project. It cannot be taken care of in isolation during the definition phase and then abandoned. Your role as controller and leader requires ongoing, unending communication—to dissolve weak links, to soothe conflicts, and to revise the schedule.

Although primarily designed as a working document for team members, your network diagram also serves as an aid to effective communication on all levels. For example, when discussing an upcoming schedule conflict for a team member with his or her department manager, you can use the network diagram to determine reassignment, changes in the timing of a phase, or solutions to problems. If the network diagram is too complex, it may inhibit communication rather than aid it. Because many separate tasks may be underway at the same time, anyone not accustomed to following the path of work may be confused by the diagram rather than enlightened. In these cases, creating a simplified flowchart in the top-to-bottom style familiar to most people. This is useful for explaining isolated segments such as a single phase or a task within a phase.

In addition to flowcharting tasks and identifying their deadlines, the time factor itself may be expressed in flowchart form. For example, if you have an upcoming deadline for a current phase of your project, and the department manager needs a team member to meet a department deadline during the same week, working out a schedule in flowchart form may show you how to resolve the problem.

Flowcharts help others to visualize the complex process of project management (not to mention departmental work). They can be used on many levels and in discussions of many of the communication weak links. When working with an outside resource (who might not appreciate the urgency of your deadline in a verbal discussion), the flowchart demonstrates visually that you are attempting to coordinate several efforts at the same time and that you have a series of deadlines that must be met in order to complete the project by its final deadline. The flowchart helps you to communicate a sense of urgency, which otherwise would not be possible.

The flowchart also helps outsiders appreciate the responsibility involved in managing a project. If you can simply state, "This is a tough job. I have to monitor seven people at the same time," the job may not seem too formidable to someone who has never done it. The flowchart, however, makes the problem of project management extremely visible. If you can communicate the fact that you function very much like a conductor who must make sure that each section of the orchestra comes in at exactly the right moment, you will improve your chances for cooperation and overall teamwork—even from outside areas of responsibility.

When communicating directly with your team members, the flowchart becomes a strategic tool for overcoming schedule variances.

Example: Your project is three days behind schedule and there are no free days between now and the final deadline. You and your team study the network diagram and identify some opportunities for making up the three days: A phase might be completed in one day less than the schedule indicates, or the team could put in more time.

MEETINGS WITH OTHER DEPARTMENTS AND OUTSIDE RESOURCES

You will need to meet with your team, with the executive who assigns the project, with other departments, and with outside resources—at the onset of your project, and possibly while the project is underway. The meetings should be short and limited, or you will spend so much time in discussion that the project will be delayed by an intended planning process.

Meetings held with outside resources and other departments should be held primarily to anticipate problems and overcome them. Your agenda (see Figure 10-2) should be designed with these six goals in mind:

1. *Express the goals of the project.* Never forget the ultimate goal of your project. You may need to communicate this goal more than once

Figure 10-2.   Agenda: meeting with outsiders.

1. **Express the goals of the project.**

2. **Explain the level of team commitment you need.**

3. **Specify deadlines for phases and final completion.**

4. **Identify critical phases.**

5. **Point out the likely problem areas.**

6. **Agree on priorities for the project.**

and to remind outside resources of what you are trying to achieve. Keeping the goal at the forefront of your discussions helps avoid sidetracking your agenda, and is an effective way to confront problems, defuse arguments, and avoid conflict. A goal orientation keeps the discussion on track.

2. *Explain the level of team commitment you need.* You may face a confrontation with a department manager concerning the time demands on an employee. The best response is not to argue but to explain the time demands of the project. There are a number of alternatives— reassignment, schedule changes, or extended deadlines. The problem, though, should never be reduced to a struggle. You want to promote a joint effort to solve a mutual problem to everyone's satisfaction.

3. *Specify deadlines for phases and final completion.* Avoid surprises when dealing with other departments or outside resources. If you are faced with the argument "You didn't tell me," either you did not communicate an upcoming deadline or, if you did, the message didn't get through.

4. *Identify critical phases.* Emphasize to outside departments and other resources which deadlines are least flexible, thus pivotal to the schedule. That way, you will improve your chances for staying on schedule throughout the project period.

5. *Point out the likely problem areas.* Don't wait for someone else to discover problems. Anticipate them and verbalize your concern. Other managers appreciate this, and will respect your consideration. For example, you may state, "In this phase, I will depend on the employee from your department. But I think the phase comes up during your busy cycle." As long as you and the other manager work together, you can resolve the problem before the conflicting deadlines are upon you. This does away with the scheduling problem, and improves your relationship with the other manager.

6. *Agree on priorities for the project.* Some project managers attempt to meet deadlines and create an atmosphere of teamwork and cooperation, only to face unending conflict—between team members, outside resources, and other departments. This problem often arises because the priorities of the project have never been expressed clearly.

Once you get other people to agree to your priorities, your communication task becomes much easier. In many projects, however, the perceptions of the various people and departments involved are so different that efforts are constantly in conflict with one another. For example, your priority may be to gather information needed to prepare a report, whereas another manager's priority is to put cost-cutting measures into effect. What is the project supposed to achieve?

Leave nothing unexplained, or assumptions will fill the gaps. If you are to get any cooperation at all, it's up to you to explain what you're doing so that it's understood by everyone involved.

RUNNING THE MEETING

You may think of meetings as long, drawn-out exercises in discussion leading to few results or decisions. Or, you may view them as simply an inefficient way to get things done. However, a well-organized and controlled meeting—especially a short one—can improve communication on all levels.

Your first task is to control the scope and time of the meeting, as follows:

1. *Invite only those who are absolutely essential to the agenda.* The more people in your meeting, the more difficult it will be to stay on the subject and to get anything done.
2. *Limit the time.* If your meetings run too long, you won't achieve results.
3. *Set meeting goals for yourself.* Write out an agenda—not just by topics but by goals. What do you want to accomplish in your meeting? Someone should be able to read the agenda and know exactly what will be achieved.

Next, you will need to get your message across to the attendees—whether team members, department managers, executives, consultants, or other outside resources. You maintain control of the meeting by moving through the agenda and ensuring that decisions are made and actions assigned. Some projects are helped by periodic five-minute team meetings, during which the coming week's assignments are discussed and clarified. Other meetings can be useful for resolving problems at various levels.

You will get your message across by using several aids to communication, such as:

1. *The agenda.* The agenda itself can be a powerful communication tool, if correctly designed. For example, a team member is facing a department deadline that interferes with a project deadline. You could list this agenda item as "Scheduling Conflicts," a passive approach. But it would be better to describe it as "Resolution to Upcoming Conflict in Schedule," thus emphasizing a solution to the problem, rather than merely raising the topic and talking about it.

2. *Simplified flowchart.* Many people have problems understanding something as complex as a network diagram. They can relate better to a top-to-bottom flowchart that isolates a period of time and a limited number of tasks or phases.

3. *Gantt chart.* To explain a scheduling problem and make it extremely visual, the Gantt chart—although not so useful for your project control effort—can be used in project meetings, if only to communicate the problem you're facing.

4. *Network diagram.* For team meetings, the network diagram is the most effective communication tool. If you expect a problem in the near future, both the explanation and the likely solution will be made easier with the use of the network diagram.

In all phases of project management, the degree to which you are able to communicate priorities determines the success of the effort. Identifying problems well in advance of their occurrence, expressing an understanding of someone else's priorities, and being able to confront issues rather than people are all attributes of the effective communicator and successful project manager.

Your ability to overcome the communication challenge will affect your role as a corporate employee and manager, as well as your participation in the role of project manager. In Chapter 11, you will see how successful project management has a positive effect on your career.

WORK PROJECT

1. Explain the communication challenge on three levels:
   a. The assignment
   b. Other departments
   c. Outside resources
2. Describe three ideas for improving communication when working with other departments.
3. List three goals to include on your agenda for a project meeting with another department.

11

Project Management and Your Career

Success is the reward of anyone who goes looking for trouble.

—Walter Winchell

"I think our manager is burning out," one project team member told another.

The second one answered, "I've noticed that he's been a bit short-tempered lately."

"That's not what I mean," the first one said. "Yesterday, he sent me down to the lunchroom to get him a cup of coffee."

"What's wrong with that?"

"Instead of just giving me a list, he drew out the instructions on a network diagram."

Who gets promoted in your company? Is it the person who is merely capable, who doesn't make waves, and who survives without upsetting the delicate balance of the corporate culture? Or is it the person who excels?

Because the "survivor" is not a risk taker, in the long term, it is the exceptional manager who receives the promotions and creates a permanent career. Whether your performance as a department manager is exceptional, or only average, if you also manage projects, you have the opportunity to exceed the "average" category.

150

In many departments, budgets, staff, tasks, and other factors will limit your freedom to demonstrate leadership abilities. You may have to struggle just to maintain the minimum requirements of the job. There may be few opportunities to demonstrate your skill, or even to put it to the test. When a project comes along, it's your opportunity to manage in a more creative way, and it allows you to develop a greater skills level than you'd ever need as a department manager.

AN ORGANIZATIONAL SCIENCE

A large part of your success as a project manager will depend on your ability to organize and define. In comparison, the actual work is not difficult. In fact, the better you do the job of organization, the easier it will be to execute the task of the project.

Organizing the project requires several leadership actions, including:

- *Defining the purpose and goals of the project.* Getting to the point of understanding between you and the person giving you a project assignment may require a great deal of effort on your part. Many people, including executives, have difficulty defining exactly what they want. Thus, you may be assigned a project, but with no clearly defined purpose or goal.

Your first organizational challenge is to ask the right questions at the point of assignment. You need to know exactly what the assignment is meant to achieve.

- *Organizing a schedule.* Once a schedule is completed, it might look like a fairly simple document: each phrase has been broken down and defined; deadlines have been made clear; and tasks have been assigned to each team member. But a complex and lengthy project will demand a high level of organizational skill in the beginning. You need to be aware of the time demands for each phase, as well as the time restrictions for your team members. You also need to look far ahead to make sure that your deadlines do not conflict with other deadlines.

- *Developing a team approach.* Your ability to lead a project team effectively depends on how well your team works together. This does not happen without focused, motivated leadership. Simply creating a team does not ensure that it will function as you want it to. The better able you are to organize all aspects of the project, the easier it will be to develop your team.

■ *Resolving conflicts.* Invariably, the time demands of your project, the schedule, and the use of resources will create conflicts at some point. Many of these relate to time priority for team members. You may need to act in the capacity of a corporate diplomat to resolve these conflicts, while at the same time avoiding power confrontations or ill feelings.

■ *Keeping the lines of communication open.* As a project manager, you will need to continually define, redefine, and modify. You must also reassure other people: team members, other department managers, outside resources, and top management. Your project team does not operate in isolation, so you must function as organizer and operator of a network of conflicting interests and priorities.

■ *Meeting budgets and deadlines.* An organized project manager needs to review status day by day by tracking the budget, looking for signs of emerging variances, and then taking action to control them. You will monitor each phase as it proceeds, with an eye on immediate and final deadlines. You will use many tools to organize your monitoring, such as PERT/CPM and network diagrams.

■ *Training and supervising.* While the project is underway, you may need to supervise team members directly. Some of them may not know how to execute a task, and will require training while working on the project.

ATTRIBUTES OF PROJECT LEADERSHIP

Achieving the many organizational goals while you work as a project manager places many demands on you—and your leadership skills. In some departments, "participative" management is not always possible nor practical; but in project management, it's essential.

Example: A manager of a processing department must ensure that transactions are executed, errors are caught and corrected, and deadlines are met. Her task is specific. There is little opportunity for employee involvement in her relatively mechanical supervisory job. However, when she's given a project with a team of expert employees, her leadership style changes: In this situation she coordinates efforts and encourages people to become involved in the process of developing the schedule, determining the sequence of phases, and overcoming problems of scheduling and budgeting.

You will succeed as a project manager when:

1. *You understand and practice the team approach.* Some people endorse participative management but don't really understand how it works. To succeed as a project manager, you need to understand and practice team participation. Once you have created the team, it needs to function in a more flexible manner than a department.

2. *You apply a standard that is different from the one used in managing your department.* Some extremely capable department managers do not succeed in running projects, mainly because they cannot make the transition. Project management is *not* the same as managing a department, and you need to approach the project team with participation in mind. You should remain in control, of course, but you also need to encourage a more democratic approach than you can in your department.

3. *You can organize a multiple effort.* On a complex project, team members operate on several phases and levels at the same time. You need to organize the concurrent effort, supervise everyone, and monitor the schedule and budget—all at the same time. You may also need to supervise and train some team members on the job. At the same time, you must continue full-time management of your department.

4. *You are flexible.* Even the best plans may change, for any number of reasons beyond your control. Whenever you function as a project manager, be prepared for unexpected changes—in the schedule, in resources, and in the purpose and goal of the project itself.

5. *You communicate well with everyone.* You might be deeply involved in the hands-on work of the project, supervising team members, and monitoring the schedule and budget. But you are still responsible for

keeping the lines of communication open—between members and with other departments, outside resources, and top management.

TAKING CHARGE

Living up to the standards for success as a project manager may seem to require a superhuman effort. The demands of supervision and communication—all needed to execute an exception to your normal routine—place considerable pressure on you. However, the solution is not to put in more hours and effort but to work to define your goals and then execute them. Do this in a realistic and orderly manner. Successful completion of a project is not measured in hours but in organizational ability.

Just as staying in control in your department requires a firm hand, you succeed in project management when you adopt a more flexible leadership style. You should determine that style according to a number of variables:

1. *The makeup of the team.* With a relatively small team, made up entirely of employees from your department, your style of leadership remains constant. But as soon as the team is expanded to include other employees, your style should be modified. A variety of team members requires that you apply a different standard.

2. *Scope of the project.* Some projects are designed to function only as committees, put together to investigate, compile, and report. Other projects lead to implementation of major changes, and may extend over many months. The style you bring to the team should be based on the scope and complexity of the project itself.

3. *Cooperation from other departments.* We would all like to believe that other department managers will cheerfully cooperate with our efforts. But in reality, this does not always occur. Thus, your management style will change depending on the people with whom you must communicate, negotiate, and compromise.

4. *Time demands.* You may need to execute a project under extreme time constraints. In some companies, this is the norm. The greater the

pressure to achieve the end result, the less luxury you have to experiment with new and more flexible management styles.

How you take charge of your project depends largely on your experience. As you go through the process of managing projects, you will find out what works and what doesn't. The circumstances unique to each project will dictate how well a technique works, and which techniques don't work.

ELIMINATING COMMON PROBLEMS

Even when you organize and lead your projects well, you may find yourself running into the same problems time and again. Learning how to resolve these difficulties will improve your chances of becoming an effective project manager. Ten common problems and their solutions are listed here:

1. *The team doesn't work well together.* When you struggle to create a team but don't succeed, first examine your own management style. Do you truly offer team members an opportunity to participate? Or do you discourage them from speaking out, offering ideas, or suggesting changes? Teams work only when you encourage participation and then follow up on it.

The problem may also be caused by excessive diversity in the team. If you have the chance to pick your own team, try to limit as much as you can the involvement of a large number of other departments. Projects often demand help from people other than those you supervise directly, but it is not always necessary to strive for participation beyond those resources you absolutely need.

2. *Other managers resist having their employees recruited to your team.* You face a formidable task just in getting cooperation from other department managers—no matter how diplomatically you approach them or how well you define and explain the project. To solve this problem, you will need to convince the other managers that their priorities will be respected.

3. *Management skills that work in the department don't seem to work on the project.* Be aware of the important differences between departmental and project management. They often require different levels of supervision and leadership. In fact, skills that work for you as a department manager may interfere with team participation, so you will probably need to develop a completely different approach to supervising the project team.

4. *The goals of the project are not well-defined.* Your first responsibility is to ensure that the goals of the project are clearly and specifically spelled out—even when the assignment is not clear. You may have to push for definition, since often the person making the assignment does not even know what he or she wants. However, don't proceed until you find out. Otherwise, your success will be a matter of chance, not of science.

5. *Top management changes the scope of the project after it has started.* Unfortunately, priorities change. You cannot always assume that a project assigned today will be valid by its deadline. Chronic changes in project assignments are a sign of poor leadership at the top, and there is little you can do while trying to accomplish an ever-changing goal.

Your solution: Continue to communicate while you are working on your project. Don't abandon communication after the initial purpose and goals have been defined. Meet weekly with the person who assigned the project and present a brief status report. Restate the goals to make sure they're still valid. Also recognize the fact that changes can also occur because of new priorities resulting from perceptions about the market, the competition, and profitability.

6. *Communication with top management while the project is underway is not effective.* How do you handle the problem of poor communication with top management? Even when you make the effort to keep the lines of communication open, management may simply fail to keep you up-to-date on priorities.

Your solution: You cannot force top management to improve their communication skills, but you can do your best to present status reports, ask for continuing definition, and convey information to the top—even if your only avenue is the interoffice memo. If you can't even get an executive to take time for a brief meeting, chances are your communication link will suffer. You may find that management does not respond to your requests or suggestions, fails to confirm project goals, and offers little support; but when the project is completed, you are told that "this is not what we wanted."

In most cases, management wants to support you, and will try to maintain morale. So even though the problems seem formidable, if you make an effort to communicate, they can usually be resolved—even if you have to train top management in the development of communication skills!

7. *The schedule is difficult to control.* Coordinating the many ongoing efforts of your team members and successfully completing many different phases within the same limited time period may be a struggle. If so, examine the method you are using to develop and control your schedule. You may have to invest more time in developing a detailed network diagram and showing team members how to use it as a control document. Most instances of scheduling control problems are created by a lack of preparation in creating the schedule itself.

Your solution: Revise your methods.

8. *Deadlines are not being met, and projects are completed late.* You may have an excellent process for schedule control, and team members are working well together. But in spite of that, you simply don't meet phase deadlines, and projects aren't completed on time.

Your solution: Allow more time, or increase the size of your team. Your schedule is not realistic, and phases cannot be executed at the pace built into it. You may have been forced to accelerate your schedule because management imposed an early deadline. When you first organize your schedule, the realistic completion time will be dictated by the scope of the job. If the final deadline is unrealistic, convey this fact to management, explain why there is a problem, and ask for a later deadline or a larger project team.

9. *Project budgets don't work, resulting in expense overruns.* In your preoccupation with schedules, it's easy to overlook the importance of the budget. Because the company's risk is defined by the financial investment it has made in the project versus the potential reward derived (either from reduced costs and expenses or increased profits in the future), the budget should be controlled very conscientiously.

When you experience budget overruns, there are two possible reasons. First, the budget may be unrealistic. In that case, you need to ask for a more suitable one. Second, you may need to exercise more direct control. Review expense levels more frequently, compare budget and actual expenses, and look for emerging variance trends. Then identify what you need to do to correct the problem and take action.

10. *There is no time for overview or control.* You may find yourself committed so heavily to tasks and supervisory duties (as well as your ongoing departmental responsibilities) that you don't have time to monitor schedules and budgets.

Your solution: No matter how busy you are, don't overlook the critical importance of overseeing your team. Project management involves several roles—trainer, supervisor, leader, and communicator. But your most important task is to control the project network. You are the organizer, the driving force that ensures that the project succeeds in every respect. Overseeing should be your highest priority. Don't become so involved in other pressures that you overlook this important fact.

MAXIMIZING YOUR SKILLS

As you gain skill in managing projects, your career prospects will improve as well. Management recognizes success and rewards it, and projects are an excellent forum for demonstrating your leadership abilities.

In addition to developing the skills required for project management, set career goals for yourself as a project manager. Recognize that management will review your performance based on how well you achieve these goals, which may include:

1. *Acquiring the reputation as a skilled, effective project manager.* Be aware that your reputation within the company will affect your career. A positive reputation includes the element of reliability. To become a *skilled* project manager, practice the ideas and techniques that make the process work. To become an *effective* project manager, keep your goals and deadlines in mind at all times, support your team, and work well with all resources, internal and external.

2. *Meeting deadlines, without fail.* Some people accept the fact that deadlines in their companies are not taken very seriously. Don't allow

yourself to think in this way. View the deadline as an absolute. If you never miss a deadline (except in the most extreme circumstances), management will think of you as a dependable, valuable resource.

3. *Staying within budget.* The budget, like the deadline, is often seen as an outmoded practice, as an idea with little validity. This is because so few people use budgets as they are intended—as control tools for measuring the effectiveness of management's effort. The budget defines risk and potential reward for the organization, and should be carefully monitored and controlled while the project is underway.

4. *Producing and delivering the desired result.* Once you have achieved a clear and precise definition of your purpose and goals, you will know exactly what management expects from you. And as long as you keep communicating to ensure that the goals have not changed, you will succeed. Produce and deliver the desired result, and management will think of you as a results-oriented manager.

5. *Resolving conflicts.* Conflicts—whether involving mere scheduling problems or personality clashes—may seem trivial in the scheme of things. But in some respects, your ability to resolve conflicts without difficulty may be the most important attribute for successful project management. You certainly want to draw attention to yourself as an effective manager; what you don't need is the kind of attention you get when top management has to step in to mediate an unresolved problem.

Opportunities for promotion will certainly come up in your company. Management will seek the individual who, in their opinion, is most qualified to fill a vacant post. However, job skills are often secondary to the less tangible attributes such as ability to lead, resolve conflicts, and produce the results that management wants—on time and within budget.

As a project manager, your opportunities to demonstrate these attributes may lead to career advancement, even more than will your performance as a department manager. When you accept an assignment, remember that top management will develop a perception of you based on your performance, the results you produce, and the conflicts you resolve quietly. You don't need a high profile in order to succeed. You can achieve more with a very low, but extremely successful, profile. You will know you're on the right track when management comes to you when they have a difficult job, and when they need it to be done quickly and professionally.

WORK PROJECT

1. Describe three types of leadership action required to organize a project.
2. Explain three skills you need to master in order to succeed as a project manager.
3. List two variables that will affect your project leadership style.

Appendix
Work Project Answers

CHAPTER 1

1. For most managers, projects and routines can be clearly distinguished from one another:
   a. In projects, functions are an exception to the normal responsibilities of the department. Routines, in comparison, are defined by the scope of the department's function within the company.
   b. The activities of a project are related to one another in some way. Routines, though, are related to one another (again, within the scope of the department's function).
   c. Project goals and deadlines are specific and finite. Routine goals and deadlines tend to be general and perpetual.
   d. A project's end result is identified specifically. Routines, though, are undertaken as part of the course of work and are not aimed at a specific end result.
2. The three constraints of every project are: result, budget, and time. Project managers are responsible for ensuring that the result is understood and agreed upon before embarking on the project. In addition, the manager needs to monitor and control the budget, and to ensure that the deadline is met. This includes not only the final deadline but deadlines for each project phase.
3. The *definition* phase of the project includes four segment:
   a. Determining the project's purpose
   b. Identifying tasks
   c. Developing a schedule

  d. Creating a budget

The *control* phase has five parts:

a. Putting together the project team
b. Coordinating work during each phase
c. Monitoring progress
d. Taking action to reverse unfavorable budget variances or to avoid scheduling delays
e. Completing the project on time

Both the definition and control phases must be carefully organized and put into effect. Without either of these, a project cannot be completed on time or within budget, and the desired result may not be known.

CHAPTER 2

1. The direct team structure involves direct contact between the project manager and each team member, including any assistants or primary contacts *and* each individual. This is appropriate when the team is limited in numbers, and when there is no need to delegate to middle levels. The direct team structure reduces bureaucracy; it is simple; and direct contact reduces the chances of misunderstanding and misdirection.

2. The organizational team structure is appropriate for teams with many members. A project leader may need to delegate responsibility to middle ranks and create a manageable system. Otherwise, too much time will be spent in details, and the important monitoring and control functions may suffer as a result. The manager does not have to sacrifice direct contact in an organizational team structure; however, responsibility for execution of phase tasks is assigned to middle levels.

3. The agenda for the initial project meeting should be designed to set the tone and create a participative environment. The agenda may include:

a. *A list of problems the team will solve.* Your initial list may be expanded through discussions with team members.
b. *Solutions the team should reach.* Again, team participation may

increase the overall value of the project, by the group's identification of additional or alternative solution paths.

c. *Information the team will need.* You may be aware of several sources for raw data or completed reports useful to your team; and the team may be able to offer additional ideas that will save time and effort.

d. *Initial assignments.* You probably will have a fairly good idea of who should execute specific tasks or take charge of project phases. But remember, team members have recurring deadlines and tasks to complete in addition to project work. Members may want to propose assignment shifts.

e. *Advance planning.* Map out responsibilities for every phase of the project in advance, but make sure that they are subject to modification later. At this point, your goal should be to ensure that the team is complete and that you have resources available to complete each phase on time.

CHAPTER 3

1. Having a project team imposed rather than being allowed to select it on your own is a difficult way to begin your project. When this occurs, consider these steps:

    a. Suggest a different approach. Talk to your boss or the person who gave you the project assignment, and explain why you think it's important to be involved in picking your team—subject to approval from above.

    b. Do your best with what you are given. Even when the team is not the right team, give it your best effort. If the decision has been made, all you can do is make the most of it.

    c. Give team members the chance to excel. If you just assume that someone can't handle an area of responsibility, you miss the chance to help others develop their skills.

    d. Request team members who work out well. If you work with someone on a project and he or she does the job you expect, remember that person the next time. Ask to have him or her included on your next project team.

   e. Ask to take part in the selection process. You might not be allowed to pick your team with complete independence; but a compromise is possible if management will listen to your ideas and recommendations.

   f. Suggest that department managers be involved as well. The team member's immediate supervisor should be included in the selection process.

2. An area of responsibility includes a range of tasks that fall within a defined skill level. An employee may be especially suited for analytical, interpretive, research, or creative work, for example. This approach differs from merely assigning tasks in these ways:

   a. The project is defined not just by its phases but by the type of effort. Team members will better understand the desired end result when they're made responsible for it.

   b. Areas of responsibility are matched to an individual's skills and interests. You can expect better results and response when you acknowledge strengths, rather than just giving out tasks to a resource pool.

   c. The area of responsibility approach provides incentives by allowing team members to assume a sense of ownership over a phase or range of related tasks.

3. The outside department must be assumed to have higher priority than your project, because:

   a. You need the other manager's support. Be ready to express your appreciation of the department's tasks, and recognize that assigning an employee to your project team may create hardships for the other manager.

   b. The department's work is permanent, while yours is temporary. A project has a finite life, but the work of a department goes on month after month. From an employee's point of view, his or her routine *is* a higher priority. You need to recognize and accept this.

   c. Departmental tasks recur and often are tied to deadlines. The work one department performs may affect other departments—and their deadlines as well. Even when you believe your deadlines *are* more critical than the department's, concede the point. Anticipate problems well in advance of the critical date, and work with the department manager to find a satisfactory resolution.

CHAPTER 4

1. The percentage-of-completion shows your estimate of each phase's portion of the total, based on labor expenses. This is a valid approach when labor (both internal and external) represents most of your project expenses. To calculate, divide the hours in each phase by the total estimated project hours:

Phase	Hours	Percentage	Cumula-tive Percentage
1	28	10%	10%
2	63	24	34
3	76	29	63
4	97	37	100
Total	264	100%	

2. To calculate the dollar cost, multiply each team member's hourly rate of pay by the budgeted hours in each phase:

Team Member	Hourly Cost	Phase 1	Phase 2	Phase 3	Phase 4
1	$20	$200	$300	$300	$500
2	15	120	120	90	180
3	18	0	270	450	360
4	9	0	180	180	225
5	10	100	50	100	150
Total		$420	$920	$1,120	$1,415

3. Nonlabor expenses can be budgeted on the percentage-of-completion method, tied to labor. However, an adjustment will be required if and when nonlabor costs do *not* follow the labor trend closely. On the assumption that expenses in this case will follow the labor trend, calculate each phase's expense by multiplying the completion percentage by the total of $2,800:

Phase	Percentage	Amount
1	10%	$ 280
2	24	672
3	29	812
4	37	1,036
Total	100%	$2,800

CHAPTER 5

1. The following points should be kept in mind when confronting delays:
   a. Every delay affects scheduling for the remainder of the project. Thus, if the first five phases are delayed by two working days each, you are likely to miss your final deadline by two weeks.
   b. To meet your deadline, the delay will have to be absorbed in a later phase. It's unlikely that you will have the luxury of time on your side. Many projects are assigned under great pressure for the final result. You need to plan ahead to absorb delays, even for the least flexible schedule.
   c. It's desirable to meet the final project deadline, unless that will mean the outcome will be incomplete, inaccurate, or short of the desired result. While meeting the promised deadline is important, you will also want to ensure that the results are of the highest quality and that the assignment is met. You may need to request an extension to achieve this goal.
   d. Staying on schedule and meeting the deadline is the project manager's job. That means you need to track every phase—not only to deal with delays as they occur but to anticipate and solve problems *before* they result in schedule delays.
2. Phases 1, 2, and 3 could be executed during the same time span. Even though it may be necessary to define these as separate phases, you can get your team working together to meet your deadline for the first three phases. The same argument can be applied to phases 5 and 6, in which revised numbers and related revisions to supporting worksheets can be executed at the same time.

3. Solutions may include the following actions:
   a. Execute phases concurrently, even if your original plan called for consecutive scheduling. There may be instances in which all or part of a phase can be executed even when previous work has not been completed.
   b. Double up your team's effort to absorb the previous delay. This might be necessary when your final deadline is approaching. An original schedule is revised so that phased deadlines get back on track.
   c. Begin preliminary steps on future phases to save time later. You might be able to save time by filling in the blanks—preparing worksheets, finding outside information, or completing part of a report.
   d. Seek methods to speed up later phases, without losing quality. For example, you may save time identifying math errors by placing information in a spreadsheet program, by reducing the planned time span of a test, or by replacing time-consuming steps with more thorough checking procedures.

CHAPTER 6

1. Work Breakdown Structuring (WBS) in outline form is a starting point for more detailed scheduling activities. Three benefits are:
   a. It enables you to identify responsibility by team member. Once you have the outline, it is next possible to assign specific phases to individuals and to ensure that work is divided fairly among the team.
   b. It provides a means for control of time on a detailed level. From the outline, you can next estimate time requirements for each phase while identifying concurrent processing.
   c. The outline helps identify weak links. These are the points where work and responsibility passes from one person to the next, and are the keys to effective scheduling.
2. Project management can be achieved through automated processes, assuming you follow these guidelines:
   a. Solve the problem of management over projects as a first step.

You cannot replace this all-important responsibility with a computer.
b. Identify recurring processes that might be better handled on a computer. Don't assume that *all* project management tasks must be automated; you may find that only a limited number of routines (those taking much of your time) can be more efficiently managed through automation, while other, less tangible routines are better handled manually.
c. Automate for processing efficiency, not to replace direct involvement. The relationship between a manager and the team can never be reduced to computerized processing. Computers can provide great efficiency for managing information, but they do not replace human communication.
d. Don't confuse project objectives and automation objectives. The project schedule, budget, and deadline are achieved by team effort; the computer is only a tool in achieving results.
e. Don't change procedures in response to program limitations. Remember, your priorities include getting the results you design as part of your management technique. If you sacrifice those priorities because a specific program can't handle them, then you defeat the intended purpose of automation.
f. Develop a practical, effective system for managing your projects manually. Once this step is complete, you can next look for ways to improve efficiency. That may involve changing a manual procedure or automating the more labor- and time-intensive routines.
3. Setting rules for flowcharting methods helps clear up the confusion often encountered when trying to reduce a complex procedure to graphic form. These rules will help:
a. The precedence method should always be used. You will clarify the task by remembering that every activity must be preceded by a logical activity or event.
b. The path of activities and events should make sense. Every process has a logical flow to it, which is identified by (1) defining exactly what the activity should achieve; (2) understanding what's needed to get to that point; and (3) knowing what will come next.
c. An activity cannot occur until a preceding activity or event has been completed. Within each path, this rule should be remembered when setting the schedule. If, in the interest of making up a

variance, you accelerate processes in violation of this rule, you will not solve the problem.

d. Concurrent events should be carefully plotted, explained, and controlled. Your team may be involved in two or more ongoing phases at the same time, which is a challenge to your organizational abilities. Assume responsibility for planning, explaining, and supervising concurrent action.

e. Control of weak links is the key to successful project management. If you concentrate on ensuring successful passage of information and responsibility from one person to another, you will avoid the majority of scheduling problems you're likely to encounter in your projects.

f. Decision steps should be flowcharted with great care to avoid confusion. A decision point, where a "yes" answer leads in one direction, and a "no" answer leads in another (or to a repeat of a previous step), may also cause delays within a phase, or confuse the team member. Accompany decision points with narrative explanations, work directly with the involved team member, and supervise the decision point to ensure its timely and successful completion.

CHAPTER 7

1. An activity includes all of the action steps required to complete phases of the project, including research, interpretation, and report preparation. An event is the result—the report itself, the document that describes new procedures, or a written summary of a department's paper flow.

    a. The action of preparing a report is an activity, and the final report itself is an event.

    b. Receiving a report from another department is an event, which leads to the activity of developing statistical summaries. Once those summaries have been completed, it's a subsequent event.

    c. When each division submits its sales activity information, those are a series of events. These are necessary in order to complete the activity of describing the reporting problem.

2. Vertical flowcharting may be a necessary step in defining the logical sequence of phases. However, this method provides very little for scheduling control and involves several flaws. The flaws of vertical flowcharting are:

   a. It doesn't provide you with the time requirements of each phase; thus, you have no means for controlling the schedule. Control, of course, is the essential element you will need to run the project. The network diagram solves this problem by linking every activity with a time standard.

   b. It doesn't provide a breakdown by area of responsibility, meaning you cannot show how the team will divide up the effort. No one team member's activities will be broken down in isolation. The network diagram shows the entire picture of activity, as well as isolating areas of responsibility by line.

   c. It doesn't break out concurrent activity as well as a Gantt chart, making it difficult to control multiple efforts during a single phase. This is desirable for control, both of individual team activities and the larger question of making the final deadline. The network diagram is perfectly suited to even the most complex project, because concurrent activities are shown on a single page *and* by area of responsibility. This is a more substantial benefit.

3. Weak links are the points in your schedule where delays are most likely to occur, usually as the consequence of poor communication. This is the greatest jeopardy to the smooth and continued operation of the entire project, and it occurs at any point where information and effort pass from one person or department to another. The network diagram helps you to control the schedule by making every weak link as visible as possible. With other scheduling methods, not every weak link will be obvious from a review of the activity diagram. Whenever all of the weak links are highlighted, you have a better chance of anticipating the need for control.

CHAPTER 8

1. This series of activities involves two people, so it should be divided into two separate sections. One solution is:

Team member 1

a. Prepare an outline of
   tasks and give it to
   team member 2.

b. Team member 2 asks
   for clarification.
   Review the outline
   and clarify.

Team member 2

a. Check the outline
   submitted by team
   member 1.

b. Is the outline clear?
   If not, ask team
   member 1 for help.

c. When team member 1
   has answered your
   questions, return
   to previous step
   (check outline).

d. The outline is clear.
   Proceed to the next
   step.

e. Prepare a flowchart
   summarizing the steps
   in this procedure.

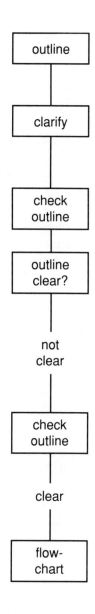

2. Loops are points in the network diagram where a positive or negative decision must be made:

   a. Verification loops ask questions that are answered by "correct" or "incorrect" responses. For example, an activity calls for checking the math on a worksheet. If correct, the team member proceeds to the next activity. If incorrect, he or she returns to a previous activity to make corrections.

   b. A decision loop is answered by a "yes" or a "no." For example, a rough draft of a form is designed and submitted to the project manager for review. A "yes" response (approval) will lead to the next activity. A "no" response (changes needed) will lead the team member back to the drafting phase.

   c. A repetition loop is used when one activity is repeated a number of times. It is characterized by the answer "complete" or "not complete." For example, an activity calls for documenting the tasks performed by each of three employees in a department. This activity is complete only when it has been repeated three times.

3. An area of responsibility should not be difficult to define. As project manager, you should have a very clear idea of which team members will take care of which phases, and where they will work together. There are three methods for arriving at definition:

   a. *Type of work.* A specific activity will require exposure to a department or to information to be found there. For example, writing processing routines for an automated system is a specific type of work, and it will dictate who will be responsible.

   b. *Individuals.* Certain people are selected for your team because of their knowledge or experience, or because of special talents they have demonstrated in past projects. For example, one of the employees in your department has a special ability for organizing and summarizing a large body of information. That person should be assigned the organizational phases of the project.

   c. *Phases.* Some phases of your project will dictate who should execute them. For example, you may write the final report on your own, as a compilation of the efforts your team contributes.

CHAPTER 9

1. Review in a project contains the same elements of review in your department. However, because the project is short-term, it demands more careful definition and follow-through. The three problems are:
   a. *Defining a standard for performance.* Your team members are expected to play specific roles in completing your project; you need to give them the guidelines for achieving the outcome you desire. This extends beyond the obvious budgetary and scheduling demands. Your standard may include guidelines for the quality of results, cooperation between team members, and the result of the project effort.
   b. *Finding appropriate applications of the standard.* You need to develop a test for review purposes, and to decide what your test reveals.
   c. *Deciding what actions, if any, you need to take.* Upon completing your periodic review, do you need to correct any problems, either existing or anticipated? You may need to identify a problem underlying a scheduling delay relating to teamwork, morale, or ability.
2. The project, unlike your department, involves a group of people who do not work together regularly. Their roles may not be well-defined. Review is a constant requirement, because problems may arise unexpectedly; because by the time you discover them, it may be too late to take action; and because the deadline is a constant consideration, especially in a short-term project. The exceptional nature of projects places an added demand on you that you do not expect to have in your department.
3. When reporting to management on the status of an ongoing project, include these sections:
   a. A brief description of the project.
   b. The current status of the schedule and the budget.
   c. Explanations where needed. Don't take up space with unnecessary explanations; reserve this section for current and unsolved problems.
   d. Your expectations for the future. Will the project be completed in time and within budget? If not, what are the causes, and what can

be done to overcome the problem? What delays, if any, do you anticipate between now and completion?

CHAPTER 10

1. Establishing and maintaining communication with just your team members is challenge enough. But in addition, you will need to effectively open the lines of communication with others:
   a. *The assignment:* The executive who gave you the assignment might have a much different idea than what you perceive for the project. Only by defining the purpose and goal of the project, and then communicating your perceptions to the executive, can you ensure that you are on the right track.

      A second problem arises when the assignment changes, or the executive's priorities are adjusted. This may occur without your knowledge. You need to keep in touch with the executive constantly to make sure you are still aiming at the right goal.
   b. *Other departments:* You cannot expect the manager of another department to adopt your project priorities at the expense of the continuing work in his or her department. The manager must live with a set of priorities first, and accommodate your project second. You can resolve many difficulties by keeping this in mind throughout the project, and by showing consideration when your team includes employees from that department. The same is true when another department is not part of the team but will serve only as an information source for your project.
   c. *Outside resources:* When you depend on the participation of other divisions, subsidiaries, or offices—or on outside vendors, other companies, and consultants—you will need to communicate with awareness of this one fact: *Your priorities are not shared by the outside resources.* They will not always appreciate the urgency of your request, nor the importance of your deadlines.
2. Approach the communication challenge in dealing with other departments with a checklist of steps. These should include:
   a. *Visiting the other manager before you finalize the schedule.* Make certain that your proposed schedule does not present a conflict for

him or her. If it does, be willing to alter the schedule before it's finalized. Always remember that the manager will feel left out if you don't involve him or her in your scheduling decisions.

b. *Keeping in touch while the project is underway.* The communication task is not limited to the early phases of your project. You will need to communicate regularly with all department managers whose employees either are part of your team or will provide information you need to complete the project.

c. *Working with the manager to anticipate problems.* Think of the other department as a team member, never as an adversary. You need their cooperation, and that's accomplished when you make the effort to cooperate and respect their priorities.

d. *Remaining as flexible as possible.* Other departments may be faced with unexpected demands and scheduling problems for their work. And that fact may affect your ability to stay on schedule. Many projects are characterized by constant revision. You need to maintain a flexible scheduling attitude and to make concessions to other departments.

e. *Confronting the problems, not the people.* When you must deal with outside departments, it's most likely that conflicts will arise. In this situation, you will need to meet and resolve the difficulty. However, there is a great difference between confronting people—which is counterproductive—and confronting problems—which leads to solutions that satisfy both sides.

3. Set goals and express them as part of your agenda. Look for action-oriented discussions and resolutions, and don't let your meetings end without solving the problems you express. Some guidelines:

a. Express the goals of the project. The goals define and add context to every discussion. They keep everyone on the subject, and help you avoid becoming sidetracked with issues not directly related to the project.

b. Explain the level of team commitment you need. Even when a department manager is not able to free up an employee, he or she can be made to understand the problems you face. That may lead to a compromise that solves the problem. Otherwise, you will be faced with an impasse in which each side maintains its point of view and no solution is possible.

c. Specify deadlines for phases and final completion. In many com-

panies, deadlines are not taken seriously, perhaps because they are missed so often. However, in a project, every phase deadline is critical, because the final deadline is directly affected. You will need to communicate carefully—and repeatedly—the importance of deadlines.
   d. Identify "critical" phases. A critical phase is one that must be completed before any subsequent work can proceed. In preparing a network diagram, these pivotal phases are quickly identified. You may be able to make up a delay in noncritical phases simply by speeding up work; but if a critical phase is delayed, that delay may be carried through to the very end.
   e. Agree on priorities for the project. Make sure that every team member and every outside department or resource understand exactly what your project is meant to achieve. If there has been no agreement as to definition, you may be in conflict through the entire time you work on the project.

CHAPTER 11

1. Leadership actions in a project are not the same as those you practice in your department. Remember that the project is an exception; it has a finite life, and it may involve people who do not report to you. You will need to organize your project with these actions:
   a. *Defining the goals and purpose of the project.* It may take considerable effort to get management to the point of definition. But this is critical to the project's success.
   b. *Organizing a schedule.* A complex project with many phases and outside resources has to be mapped out carefully. You should use the initial schedule to identify future conflicts and to resolve them before the schedule is finalized.
   c. *Developing a team approach.* When you draw your team together, you should encourage each member to take an active part in controlling and modifying the schedule, in meeting deadlines, and in staying within the budget. The project is an opportunity for teamwork that you may not be able to exercise in your department.

    d. *Resolving conflicts.* Problems will arise, either because of scheduling difficulties or because of personalities. As project manager, you need to anticipate these problems and resolve them with diplomacy.

    e. *Keeping the lines of communication open.* You need to be constantly aware of the network involved with your project. Team members, outside resources, other departments, and top management are all involved.

    f. *Meeting budgets and deadlines.* The project is best judged by how well you meet the standard for performance. And that is defined by the budget (financial investment) and by the schedule (time and effort and deadline).

    g. *Training and supervising.* You function not only in the role of controller and organizer but also as a project supervisor. You need to ensure that each team member understands the assignment and knows how to proceed. In some cases, close supervision or training will be part of your job.

2. You will succeed as a project manager when you master these skills:

    a. You understand and practice the team approach. You need to inspire your team to work as a single unit, while also accepting responsibility for specific phases and tasks.

    b. You apply a standard that is different from the one used in managing your department. The project, because it's an exception and a temporary effort, cannot be run in the same way as a department. Thus, as leader, you need to examine your management standards and modify your approach.

    c. You can organize a multiple effort. Your project will involve several coordinated but separate actions. Your ability to organize, with the use of a well-planned schedule, will define your leadership ability for the project.

    d. You are flexible. Projects tend to change because of emerging priorities, scheduling problems, and even changes in the project's goals. As project manager, you need to be prepared to rethink the job.

    e. You communicate well with everyone. Clarity in the message helps you to avoid the most common conflicts and missed assignments. You need to control a network that includes every team member, outside resources, other departments, and top management.

3. No single series of rules and standards can be applied to every project. Variables will affect your style:

   a. *The makeup of the team.* Some projects will include people only from your own department, while others will draw people from several other departments; you may also have to work with outside resources or consultants.

   b. *Scope of the project.* A short-term, simple project cannot be managed in the same way as a longer-term, more expensive activity. Thus, how you approach, define, and organize your project will depend on its scope.

   c. *Cooperation from other departments.* If you establish clear lines of communication and keep other managers informed (whether they are resources or have employees on your team), you minimize likely problems. However, you cannot always count on complete cooperation from others. The amount of conflict you encounter will invariably affect your management style.

Index